Crazy for Chocolate

The Confident Cooking Promise of Success

Welcome to the world of Confident Cooking,
where recipes are double-tested by our team
of home economists to achieve a high standard
of success—and delicious results every time.

bay books

C O N T E

Chocolate Yoghurt Cake, page 28

Chocolate Biscuit Shapes, page 44

Chocolate Cheesecake Slice, page 58

Chocolate Baskets with Honeycomb Ice-cream, page 62

Frozen Chocolate and Berry Chequerboard Parfait, page 70

Kirsch Chocolate Cherries, page 91

The Publisher thanks the following for their assistance in the photography for this book: Albi Imports, Country Affair, Cydonia The Glass Studio, Food Service Equipment International, Incorporated Agencies, LA Decorative Design, Piper Design, South Pacific Fabrics, Ventura Design, Villeroy & Boch, Waterford Wedgewood.

Chocolate Tuiles, page 110

All recipes in this book have been double-tested.

When we test our recipes, we rate them for ease of preparation. The following cookery ratings are on the recipes in this book, making them easy to use and understand.

A single Cooking with Confidence symbol indicates a recipe that is simple and generally quick to make – perfect for beginners.

Two symbols indicate the need for just a little more care and a little more time.

Three symbols indicate special dishes that need more investment in time, care and patience–but the results are worth it.

NOTES
International conversions and a glossary explaining unfamiliar terms can be found on page 112. Cooking times may vary slightly depending on the individual oven. We suggest you check the manufacturer's instructions to ensure proper temperature control.

Chocolate Know-how

No need to be daunted. Getting to know chocolate is one of the great pleasures of the kitchen.

WHICH CHOCOLATE TO USE?

Four categories of chocolate are used in this book:
· dark chocolate
· milk chocolate
· white chocolate
· compound chocolate
All have different chemistries and, therefore, different uses.

Dark chocolate: contains sugar, cocoa liquor or mass, cocoa butter and flavourings. It is sometimes referred to as couverture chocolate.

Milk chocolate: contains the same ingredients as dark, with the addition of milk solids.

White chocolate: contains a mixture of sugar, full cream milk, cocoa butter and flavourings.

Compound chocolate: contains all of the ingredients of chocolate, with the addition of vegetable fats—which allows it to set relatively quickly, and at room temperature. Chocolate 'melts' (available in dark, milk and white forms) are compound chocolate.

The recipes in this book specify which type of chocolate to use. (Generally compound chocolate cannot be substituted for couverture chocolate and vice versa.)

There are many brands of chocolate on the market and quality, both in terms of taste and ease of handling, varies enormously. Price is a good indicator of quality. Alternatively, check the ingredients listed on the packet; any chocolate containing cocoa liquor as the main (first) ingredient is best quality. Chocolate labelled 'cooking chocolate' does not differ markedly from eating chocolate, although it may contain slightly less sugar. Use whichever type you prefer.

You can make your own compound chocolate by melting chocolate and a small amount of white vegetable shortening (copha) together. Use 5 g (about $^1/_4$ oz) vegetable shortening for each 100 g ($3^1/_3$ oz) chocolate.

STORING CHOCOLATE

Store all unopened chocolate in a cool, dry place—in the refrigerator, in summer. (It may be necessary to bring the chocolate to room temperature before chopping or grating.)

Sometimes chocolate will develop a white 'bloom' on its surface. This is most usually a result of a change in the sugar chemistry or a radical temperature change, however, the bloom is harmless and does not affect its flavour; it can be melted, although it is unattractive to serve. If in doubt, taste the affected chocolate—stale chocolate (which can also develop a bloom) is unpleasant and dry. It should not be used.

Most chocolate (depending on its quality) will store for several months, even once it has been opened. Wrap in foil or cover with plastic wrap and store in a cool place. Chocolate can be frozen for six months; wrap well and remember to label.

MELTING CHOCOLATE

Although melting chocolate is not difficult in theory, probably the easiest part is working out when it has gone wrong. Chocolate either melts successfully or it doesn't. When it doesn't (and there is no mistaking it) you will have to discard the chocolate and start again. For this reason, you should practise melting chocolate at

A selection of types of chocolate: chocolate melts, block chocolate, choc bits, choc dots.

least once before trying out that spectacular new dessert.

The aim is to melt the chocolate uniformly without cooking it or burning it. Chocolate from a bar or block should be chopped, grated or slivered for even melting. (Chocolate melts, dots, bits or buttons do not need further chopping or grating—they are already an even, manageable shape; this is their advantage.)

Place the chocolate pieces in a small heatproof bowl, then stand this bowl over a pan of gently simmering water. Make sure that the base of the bowl is not sitting in the water and that the water is not boiling rapidly. Boiling water will produce steam which may combine with the melting

Use a wooden spoon to stir the chocolate occasionally as it melts.

chocolate and cause it to seize up. Stir chocolate until it has melted and the mixture is smooth.

Once the chocolate has melted work quickly to the next stage before the chocolate sets. (Compound chocolate will set at room temperature.) Try to prevent any water or steam coming into contact with the melted chocolate. A small amount of liquid, even from a wet spoon, may cause the chocolate to seize and stiffen, rendering it unusable. If this happens—the chocolate becomes a mealy, stiff substance— you will have to start again with fresh chocolate.

Once you have mastered melting a particular brand of chocolate, stick with that brand as far as practicable. Each brand of chocolate differs slightly from another and will, therefore, behave differently. Also bear in mind that the weather will affect the melting and re-setting times. Try not to expose the chocolate to extremes of temperature.

Melting in the microwave

Place the chocolate pieces in a microwave-safe bowl. Microwave, uncovered, on High in 30-second bursts, testing chocolate each time. (Melting time will depend on the amount of chocolate and the wattage of the microwave.) Microwaved chocolate will hold its external shape, even when well melted inside. The chocolate has melted when it yields to pressure from a spoon and can be worked into liquefied form. Do not microwave chocolate until it melts on the outside, as it will be burned on the inside.

DECORATING WITH CHOCOLATE

Once you have mastered one or two decorations, you can vary the shapes and sizes. Experiment by putting various decorations together—chocolate leaves can be made into a bouquet, for example, or make curls and shapes with dark, light and white chocolate in combination.

Quick Decorations

Here are some simple decorations that do not require melted chocolate.

Shavings

Use a sharp knife or vegetable peeler against a block of chocolate to produce long or short curls. Shavings are a quick and easy way to finish a dessert or cake.

When shaving chocolate, make sure the block is at room temperature.

Gratings

Use a vegetable grater to grate block chocolate onto a sheet of greaseproof paper. Gratings are often used on warm or cold chocolate drinks (see pages 8–11).

Special Decorations

These decorations require you to melt the chocolate and re-fashion it in some way. Some are simple; others are more challenging, but are worth the time and effort.

Caraque Curls

Melt 100 g ($3^1/_3$ oz) chocolate; spread a thin layer on a cool, flat surface, such

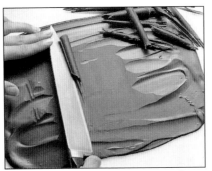

Use a sharp knife at a 45° angle to make chocolate curls.

as a marble chopping or wooden board. Using the edge of a sharp, flat knife at a 45° angle, scrape thin strips of chocolate away from your body. The strips will curl as they come away. (If the chocolate breaks, it has set too hard and must be re-melted.)

Caraque curls can be refrigerated between sheets of greaseproof paper for up to 2 weeks. Curls can also be frozen for up to 6 months.

To make fat curls: Melt chocolate and spread over flat surface. Allow the chocolate to set. Use a metal ice-cream scoop to drag the curls towards you. Varied pressure will determine the thickness of the curls.

Drizzles and Shapes

Drizzles: Spoon melted chocolate into a paper piping bag or re-useable bag fitted with a small plain nozzle. Drizzle the chocolate slowly over a sheet of greaseproof paper to form random shapes, squiggles and swirls. Allow to set before removing with a flat knife.

Shapes: Draw shapes such as stars, hearts and fans on a sheet of grease-proof paper. Pipe melted chocolate to fill or outline shape. Allow to set before removing with a flat knife.

Pipe thin lines of chocolate backwards and forwards over a rolling pin.

Zig-zags: Wrap a rolling pin or bottle with baking paper. Pipe thin lines of melted chocolate backwards and forwards over the roll of the paper. Allow chocolate to set. Carefully peel away paper.

HOW TO MAKE A PAPER PIPING BAG

Cut a 25 cm (10 inch) square out of baking paper and fold in half diagonally to form a triangle. Working with the long side facing away

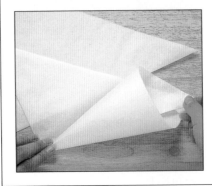

from you, pull one corner in to the centre. Hold in place while bending in the other corner and wrapping tightly to form a snug cone shape. Tuck upstanding ends inside the paper cone and fold down to secure. Spoon chocolate into bag. Fold down bag to seal. Snip off tip and gently apply pressure to force out contents. (Practice will show you how to vary the pressure to achieve the correct flow.) Discard bag once empty. (Bags still containing chocolate can be stored in a cool, dark place and microwaved 40–50 seconds to re-melt.)

A selection of chocolate decorations: cut-outs, caraque curls, fat curls, shapes, drizzles, shavings, zig-zags, chocolate leaves.

CHOCOLATE TIDBITS

➤ A brown paper bag or freezer bag can be used as an emergency piping bag. Spoon in the required quantity of chocolate and snip off a tiny corner.

➤ If a freshly baked cake seems too 'crumby' to ice, spread it with a thin layer of very soft butter and place in the freezer for 30 minutes. The icing will then stick to the butter layer.

➤ Shiny chocolate glazes can be dulled by refrigeration—the tiny drops of moisture that form on the surface damage the sheen. Rather than refrigerate desserts, such as tortes, make glazed desserts as close as possible to serving time and store in the coolest part of the house.

➤ Frozen chocolate should be thawed completely in its wrapper to prevent moisture forming on its surface.

➤ Always use clean, dry hands and utensils. Wear cotton gloves to avoid leaving fingerprints and marks on finished chocolate.

➤ A stainless steel paint scraper is ideal for cleaning counters and surfaces which have been spread with melted chocolate.

➤ Don't forget to lick the spoon when you've finished!

Chocolate Leaves

These may take some practice. Use large, well defined leaves that are free from blemishes and chemical sprays. Rose or ivy leaves are often used, although any leaves are suitable for coating (as long as they are not poisonous). Melt chocolate in a small bowl. Using a fine new paintbrush, coat the leaf evenly with chocolate. Allow chocolate to set. Apply a second coat if chocolate looks thin in parts. When chocolate has completely set, carefully prise away the leaf (not the chocolate).

Paint an even coating of chocolate over the leaf.

When chocolate has set, gently peel away the leaf.

Moulds

Variously shaped moulds can be bought from specialist outlets or department stores. Wipe with a clean tea-towel each time, then spoon melted chocolate into the shapes. Allow to set, then turn out with a gentle twisting motion as you would with a tray of ice cubes.

Cut-outs

Pour melted chocolate onto a sheet of greaseproof paper. Smooth to an even

Interesting decorations can be made with a variety of biscuit cutters.

thickness and allow to almost set. Use small sharp biscuit cutters to mark different shapes, such as stars, hearts and diamonds. You can also use plain or fluted rounds to cut out shapes.

Hot Chocolate Drinks

Sinful, nourishing, decadent or wholesome—hot chocolate in any form
is a luxury that gives warmth and comfort on a winter's night.
Use quality chocolate and Dutch or dark cocoa powder for best results.
These are available from good delicatessens and gourmet food stores.
Unless milk or white chocolate is indicated in the recipe, use good quality
dark chocolate, not compound chocolate.

CHOC-BUTTERED RUM

In a mug or heavy glass, combine 1 teaspoon each of
butter, soft brown sugar and cocoa powder. Add a
dash of dark rum and top up with boiling water,
stirring to dissolve all ingredients. Add more sugar
to taste, if necessary. Serve immediately.

WHITE HEAT

In a mug, combine 1 teaspoon cocoa powder with a
little water, and stir to make a paste. Add 1 heaped
tablespoon of chopped white chocolate and pour over
hot milk, stirring briskly until frothy.

MOCHA LATTE

Pour ¼ cup (60 ml/2 fl oz) strong black coffee into a heavy glass or mug; add 1 heaped tablespoon of cocoa powder. Heat ¼ cup (60 ml/2 fl oz) of milk without boiling; add to coffee. Serve immediately.

THE ULTIMATE HOT CHOCOLATE

Roughly chop 60 g (2 oz) dark chocolate and place in a small pan. Add 2 tablespoons water; stir over low heat until chocolate has melted. Gradually add 2 cups (500 ml/16 fl oz) hot milk, whisking until smooth and slightly frothy; heat without boiling. Pour into mugs; float one or two marshmallows on top.

SPICY HOT CHOCOLATE

Place 2–3 teaspoons of quality drinking chocolate in a mug. Add a pinch each of ground cinnamon, nutmeg and ginger; stir in a little boiling water. Pour in 1 cup (250 ml/8 fl oz) of hot milk, stirring continuously. Serve. Top with whipped cream and grated chocolate for extra richness, if desired.

LAYERED MOCHA CREAM

Pour some strong black coffee into a heavy glass; stir in 1 heaped teaspoon of drinking chocolate. Slowly pour 1 tablespoon of cream over the back of a spoon so the cream floats on top.

CLASSIC COCOA FOR TWO

Combine 1 tablespoon each of cocoa powder and sugar in a small pan. Add ¼ cup (60 ml/2 fl oz) water; whisk until smooth. Bring to the boil, reduce heat to low and add 2 cups (500 ml/16 fl oz) hot milk, whisking continuously until frothy. Serve immediately in mugs. Add a dash of rum or whisky, if desired.

Hot Chocolate Drinks are illustrated below.
Left to right: White Heat, Choc-Buttered Rum,
Mocha Latte, Layered Mocha Cream,
The Ultimate Hot Chocolate, Classic Cocoa for
Two, Spicy Hot Chocolate

Cold Chocolate Drinks

Remember a good old fashioned iced chocolate, or a frosty chocolate thickshake after a day at the beach? The kids will love to help make these drinks.

ICED CHOCOLATE

In a long glass, combine 1 tablespoon of drinking chocolate with a little milk and stir until smooth. Top with ice-cold milk. Float whipped cream or a scoop of vanilla ice-cream (or both) on top.

JAFFA FIZZ

Fill a tall glass with orange-flavoured soft drink. Top with a scoop of chocolate ice-cream; stir gently. Decorate with sliced orange.

CHOCOLATE THICKSHAKE

Place 1 cup (250 ml/8 fl oz) of milk and 1 tablespoon of chocolate syrup in a blender; process briefly to combine. Add 1–2 scoops chocolate ice-cream and blend until the mixture is smooth but not runny. (The shake should be very thick.) Pour the mixture into a large glass and serve with a wide straw.

CHOC-MINT SHAKE

Combine 2 cups (500 ml/16 fl oz) milk, 4–5 ice cubes and 6 pieces of peppermint-filled chocolate in a blender or food processor; blend until smooth. Add some ice-cream, if you like.

CHOC-BANANA SMOOTHIE

Combine 1 large peeled and sliced banana, 1 cup (250 ml/8 fl oz) milk and 1 tablespoon creamy plain yoghurt in a blender. Add a dash of chocolate syrup and blend until thick and frothy.

CHOCOLATE MALTED

Combine 1 cup (250 ml/8 fl oz) cold milk, 1 small scoop of ice-cream, a dash of chocolate syrup and 1 heaped teaspoon malted milk powder in a blender or food processor; blend until frothy. Top with chocolate gratings or shavings, if desired.

STRAWBERRY-CHOC MILK

Pour ice-cold milk into a tall glass. Add a dash of strawberry syrup and a large tablespoon of grated milk chocolate; stir to combine.

Cold Chocolate Drinks are illustrated below. Left to right: Iced Chocolate, Jaffa Fizz, Chocolate Thickshake, Choc-Mint Shake, Choc-Banana Smoothie, Chocolate Malted, Strawberry-Choc Milk

Chocktails

Chocolate is not often thought of as a cocktail ingredient, but its flavour marries well with many spirits and liqueurs—from the rich sweetness of crème de cacao to the subtle tang of Grand Marnier. The chocolate-based liqueurs—Bailey's Irish Cream or Kahlua, for example—are also delicious on their own, over ice. Cheers!

SPIKED CHOCOLATE

Combine 1 tablespoon hot water and 2 teaspoons drinking chocolate in a small glass; stir to dissolve. Cool, then add ice, 30 ml (1 fl oz) Tia Maria and 30 ml (1 fl oz) white curaçao; stir to combine. Garnish with strawberries and rose petals, if desired.

WHITE RUSSIAN

Combine ice, 30 ml (1 fl oz) vodka, 30 ml (1 fl oz) crème de cacao and 30 ml (1 fl oz) cream in a cocktail shaker; shake well. Strain into tumbler over extra ice.

BLACK FOREST

In a chilled champagne glass place a firm, ripe fresh cherry (leave the stalk on if you prefer). Pour over 30 ml (1 fl oz) each of crème de cacao and kirsch, and top with chilled champagne.

CHOCOLADA

Combine crushed ice, 60 ml (2 fl oz) white rum, 30 ml (1 fl oz) coconut cream and 2 teaspoons chocolate syrup in a tall glass; stir to combine. Garnish with sliced fresh pineapple and pineapple leaves.

BRANDY ALEXANDER

Combine ice, 30 ml (1 fl oz) brandy, 30 ml (1 fl oz) crème de cacao and 30 ml (1 fl oz) thick cream in a cocktail shaker; shake well. Strain into a martini glass; sprinkle with a little nutmeg and cocoa powder.

GRASSHOPPER

Combine ice, 30 ml (1 fl oz) crème de menthe, 30 ml (1 fl oz) crème de cacao and 30 ml (1 fl oz) cream in a cocktail shaker; shake well. Strain into a martini glass and garnish with mint leaves.

GRAND FIZZ

Combine 15 ml (½ fl oz) crème de cacao and 15 ml (½ fl oz) Grand Marnier in a champagne glass and stir to combine. Top with chilled champagne and garnish with a twist of orange.

CHOCOLATE-BASED LIQUEURS

Bailey's Irish Cream: blend of Irish whiskey, cream and chocolate. **Cleopatra:** liqueur flavoured with chocolate and orange. **Crème de cacao:** very sweet liqueur flavoured with roasted cocoa beans, vanilla and spices. It comes in white or brown forms. **Kahlua:** Mexican liqueur flavoured with coffee beans, cocoa beans, vanilla and brandy. **Royal Chocolate Liqueur:** opaque liqueur with a chocolate and peppermint flavour. **Vandermint:** Dutch liqueur flavoured with mint and chocolate.

Chocktails are illustrated below. Left to right: Spiked Chocolate, White Russian, Black Forest, Chocolada, Brandy Alexander, Grasshopper, Grand Fizz.

CAKES

ULTRA CHOC-CHIP CAKE

Preparation time: 20 minutes +
  30 minutes standing
Total cooking time: 1 hour
Makes one 20 cm (8 inch) round cake

125 g (4 oz) butter
1 cup (185 g/6 oz) soft brown sugar
1 tablespoon instant expresso
  coffee powder
2 eggs, lightly beaten
1 teaspoon vanilla essence
$1/3$ cup (40 g/$1^1/3$ oz) self-
  raising flour
1 cup (125 g/4 oz) plain flour
1 teaspoon bicarbonate of soda
$1/2$ cup (60 g/2 oz) cocoa powder
$3/4$ cup (185 ml/6 fl oz) buttermilk
$1/2$ cup (90 g/3 oz) dark choc bits

Icing
100 g ($3^1/3$ oz) unsalted butter
100 g ($3^1/3$ oz) dark chocolate,
  chopped

► PREHEAT OVEN to moderate 180°C (350°F/Gas 4). Brush a deep 20 cm (8 inch) round cake tin with melted butter or oil. Line base and sides with baking paper.
1 Using electric beaters, beat butter and sugar until light and creamy; add coffee powder. Beat until combined. Add eggs gradually, beating well after each addition; add essence.

2 Transfer mixture to large bowl. Using a metal spoon, fold in sifted flours, soda and cocoa alternately with buttermilk. Stir until combined and smooth. Stir through choc bits. Pour mixture into prepared tin; smooth surface. Bake 50–60 minutes or until skewer comes out clean when inserted into the centre of the cake. Leave cake in tin 30 minutes before turning onto wire rack to cool.
3 **To make Icing**: Melt butter and chocolate in a small heatproof bowl; stand bowl over a pan of simmering water until chocolate is smooth and glossy. When cool, spread icing evenly over top of cake. Decorate with chocolate zig-zags, if desired. (See below.)

COOK'S FILE

Storage time: Cake can be made up to 3 days ahead. Store in an airtight container.
Note: *To make Zig-Zags:* Wrap a rolling pin with baking paper. Place 100 g ($3^1/3$ oz) chocolate melts in heatproof bowl; stand bowl over pan of simmering water. Stir until chocolate has melted and mixture is smooth. Pour into paper icing bag; seal end and snip off tip. Drizzle chocolate over baking paper in zig-zag patterns. When set, carefully lift off with a flat-bladed knife. Store in an airtight container in the refrigerator, between sheets of greaseproof paper.

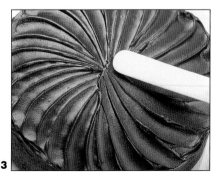

EASY CHOCOLATE AND PINEAPPLE CAKE

Preparation time: 20 minutes
Total cooking time: 35 minutes
Makes one 20 cm (8 inch) round cake

125 g (4 oz) butter
2 tablespoons cocoa powder
$^{1}/_{4}$ cup (60 ml/2 fl oz) milk
3 eggs
$^{3}/_{4}$ cup (185 g/6 oz) caster sugar
1$^{1}/_{4}$ cups (155 g/5 oz) self-
    raising flour
1 teaspoon vanilla essence
60 g (2 oz) glacé pineapple, cut
    into thin strips
2 tablespoons icing sugar
thin slices glacé pineapple, for
    decoration

➤ PREHEAT OVEN to moderate 180°C (350°F/Gas 4). Brush a deep 20 cm (8 inch) round cake tin with melted butter or oil. Line base with baking paper.

1 Combine butter, cocoa and milk in a small pan. Stir over low heat until the butter has melted and the mixture is smooth.

2 Using electric beaters, beat eggs and sugar in large bowl until thick and pale yellow in colour. Using a metal spoon, fold in sifted flour alternately with the butter and milk mixture.

3 Add vanilla essence and pineapple; stir until combined and mixture is smooth. Spoon mixture evenly into prepared tin; smooth surface. Bake for 35 minutes or until skewer comes out clean when inserted in centre.

4 Leave cake in tin 5 minutes before turning out onto wire rack to cool. Dust with icing sugar before serving and decorate with thin slices of extra glacé pineapple.

COOK'S FILE

Storage time: Once decorated, this cake should be eaten immediately. The basic cake can be made up to three days in advance. Store in an airtight container.

Variation: Other types of glacé fruit can be used in this recipe—either on their own, or in combination. Try glacé ginger, cherries, apricots, peaches, pears or oranges.

RICH FUDGE AND MARSHMALLOW CRUSTED CHOCOLATE CAKE

Preparation time: 20 minutes +
25 minutes standing
Total cooking time: 45 minutes
Makes one 23 cm (9 inch) round cake

1 cup (125 g/4 oz) plain flour
$^{1}/_{4}$ cup (30 g/1 oz) self-raising flour
$^{1}/_{4}$ cup (30 g/1 oz) cocoa powder
1 teaspoon bicarbonate of soda
$^{1}/_{2}$ cup (125 g/4 oz) caster sugar
$^{1}/_{3}$ cup (60 g/2 oz) soft brown sugar
1 egg
1 teaspoon vanilla essence
60 g (2 oz) butter, melted
$^{1}/_{2}$ cup (125 ml/4 fl oz) milk
125 g (4 oz) white mini
marshmallows

➤PREHEAT OVEN to moderate 180°C (350°F/Gas 4). Brush a deep 23 cm (9 inch) round cake tin with melted butter or oil. Line base with baking paper.

1 Sift the flours, cocoa and soda into a large bowl. Add the sugars; make a well in the centre.

2 Add combined egg, vanilla essence, butter and milk. Using a wooden spoon, stir ingredients until mixture is smooth. Stir through marshmallows.

3 Pour mixture evenly into prepared tin; smooth surface. Bake 40–45 minutes or until skewer comes out clean when inserted in centre of cake. Leave cake in tin 25 minutes before turning onto wire rack to cool. Dust with icing sugar using a template (see page 78 for instructions) before serving.

COOK'S FILE

Hint: If mini marshmallows are unavailable, use chopped larger ones.

1

2

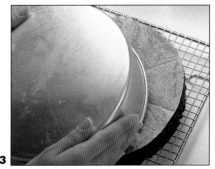
3

BANANA, NUT AND CHOC CHIP CAKE

Preparation time: 20 minutes
Total cooking time: 45 minutes
Makes one 23 cm (9 inch) ring cake

125 g (4 oz) butter
$^3/_4$ cup (185 g/6 oz) caster sugar
2 eggs, lightly beaten
$1^1/_4$ cups (155 g/5 oz) self-raising flour
1 teaspoon bicarbonate of soda
2 tablespoons milk
$^3/_4$ cup (180 g/5$^3/_4$ oz) mashed banana
$^1/_4$ cup (25 g/$^3/_4$ oz) pecan nuts, chopped
$^1/_2$ cup (90 g/3 oz) choc bits
cinnamon or nutmeg, for dusting

$^1/_3$ cup (40 g/1$^1/_3$ oz) chopped pecans, extra, for decoration

Cream Cheese Icing
125 g (4 oz) cream cheese
$^1/_4$ cup (30 g/1 oz) icing sugar, sifted
1 teaspoon vanilla essence
2 tablespoons cream

➤ PREHEAT OVEN to moderate 180°C (350°F/Gas 4). Brush a 23 cm (9 inch) fluted ring tin with melted butter or oil.

1 Using electric beaters, beat butter and sugar until light and creamy. Add eggs gradually, beating thoroughly after each addition. Transfer mixture to large bowl. Using a metal spoon, fold in sifted flour and soda alternately with milk. Stir through banana, pecans and choc bits, until just combined.

2 Spoon the mixture evenly into the prepared tin; smooth surface. Bake 40–45 minutes or until skewer comes out clean when inserted in centre. Leave cake in tin 10 minutes before turning onto wire rack to cool.

3 To make Cream Cheese Icing: Using electric beaters, beat cream cheese in small mixing bowl until light and creamy. Add icing sugar, essence and cream; beat thoroughly until well combined. Spread over cake. Sprinkle with cinnamon or nutmeg and extra pecans, before serving.

COOK'S FILE

Hint: Omit vanilla essence and cream in Icing and substitute 1 teaspoon grated orange or lemon rind and 1–2 tablespoons lemon juice, if you prefer.

GRATED CHOCOLATE CAKE

Preparation time: 40 minutes
Total cooking time: 40 minutes
Makes one 20 cm (8 inch) ring cake

1¹/₄ cups (155 g/5 oz) self-
  raising flour
³/₄ cup (185 g/6 oz) caster sugar
70 g (2¹/₃ oz) butter, melted
¹/₄ cup (60 ml/2 fl oz) water
2 egg yolks
1 teaspoon grated orange rind
1 teaspoon vanilla essence
4 egg whites
60 g (2 oz) dark chocolate, grated

Chocolate Icing
70 g (2¹/₃ oz) dark chocolate
70 g (2¹/₃ oz) butter

➤ PREHEAT OVEN to moderate 180°C (350°F/Gas 4). Brush a deep 20 cm (8 inch) ring tin with melted butter or oil.
1 Line base of tin with baking paper. Sift flour into large bowl. Add sugar; make a well in the centre.
2 Combine butter, water, yolks and rind in a jug. Using a wooden spoon, stir the butter mixture into dry ingredients; stir until combined. Add vanilla essence and stir through.
3 Place egg whites in clean dry bowl. Using electric beaters, beat until firm peaks form. Carefully fold a third of the white into cake mixture. Add remaining egg white and grated chocolate, folding lightly until the ingredients are combined.
4 Spoon mixture into prepared tin; smooth surface. Bake 40 minutes. Leave cake in tin 15 minutes before

turning onto wire rack to cool. Top the cake with Chocolate Icing.
To make Chocolate Icing: Melt chocolate and butter in heatproof bowl; stand bowl over pan of simmering water until chocolate is smooth and glossy. Cool slightly and spread the chocolate mixture over cake. Decorate cake with chocolate shavings, orange rind and dust with icing sugar, if desired. This cake is best eaten on the day it is made.

MOIST CHOCOLATE JAM CAKE WITH SPOTTED CHOCOLATE COLLAR

Preparation time: 50 minutes
Total cooking time: 45 minutes
Makes one 23 cm (9 inch) round cake

125 g (4 oz) butter
1/2 cup (125 g/4 oz) caster sugar
1 teaspoon vanilla essence
2 eggs
1/2 cup (160 g/5 1/4 oz) strawberry jam
1/3 cup (40 g/1 1/3 oz) self-raising flour
1 cup (125 g/4 oz) plain flour
1 teaspoon bicarbonate of soda
1/2 cup (60 g/2 oz) cocoa powder
3/4 cup (185 ml/6 fl oz) buttermilk
cocoa powder, for dusting

Chocolate Icing
150 g (4 3/4 oz) white chocolate melts
125 g (4 oz) butter
1/3 cup (80 ml/2 3/4 fl oz) cream

Chocolate Collar
40 g (1 1/3 oz) white chocolate melts, melted
80 g (2 2/3 oz) dark chocolate melts, melted

➤ PREHEAT OVEN to moderate 180°C (350°F/Gas 4). Brush a deep 23 cm (9 inch) round cake tin with melted butter or oil. Line base and sides with baking paper.
1 Using electric beaters, beat butter, sugar and vanilla essence in small bowl until light and creamy. Add eggs gradually, beating well after each addition. Add jam; beat until smooth.
2 Transfer mixture to large bowl.

Using a metal spoon, fold in sifted flours, soda and cocoa alternately with buttermilk. Stir until smooth. Pour mixture into prepared tin. Bake for 45 minutes or until skewer comes out clean when inserted in the centre. Leave cake in tin 5 minutes before turning onto wire rack to cool.
3 To make Chocolate Icing: Combine white chocolate, butter and cream in small pan; stir over low heat until chocolate and butter have melted and mixture is smooth. Remove from heat. Transfer to a bowl and leave to cool, stirring occasionally.
4 Place cake on serving plate; spread sides and top of cake evenly with Chocolate Icing.
5 To make Chocolate Collar: Measure the height of the cake with a ruler. (Cake should be about 6 cm/2 1/2 inches high.) Cut a long rectangular strip (75 x 6.5 cm/30 x 2 1/2 inches) out of baking paper. Drop dots of melted white chocolate randomly over strip. Allow to just set, then spread a layer of melted dark chocolate over the entire strip. Working quickly, wrap paper, chocolate-side in, around cake.
6 Hold paper strip in place until chocolate sets, then carefully peel away paper. Refrigerate cake until ready to serve. Just before serving, dust the cake heavily with sifted cocoa powder.

COOK'S FILE

Storage time: Cake can be made a day in advance. Refrigerate until needed and serve at room temperature.
Variations: White chocolate can be coloured with oil-based food colouring to make coloured dots on the collar.

Flavour white chocolate icing with finely grated orange, lemon or lime rind, or add 1 tablespoon of a colourless liqueur, such as Cointreau.

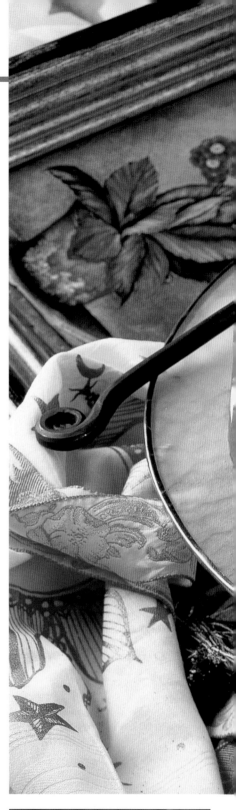

1

2

3

4

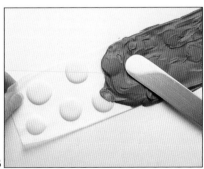
5

6

CHOCOLATE RUM & RAISIN CAKE

Preparation time: 20 minutes +
  1 hour standing
Total cooking time: 1 hour 15 minutes
Makes one 20 cm (8 inch) round cake

$1/4$ cup (60 ml/2 fl oz) hot water
2 tablespoons dark rum
$1/3$ cup (40 g/$1^1/3$ oz) raisins,
  finely chopped
$1^1/3$ cups (165 g/$5^1/2$ oz) self-
  raising flour
$1/3$ cup (40 g/$1^1/3$ oz) plain flour
$1/3$ cup (40 g/$1^1/3$ oz) cocoa
  powder
$3/4$ cup (185 g/6 oz) caster sugar
$1/4$ cup (55 g/$1^3/4$ oz) demerara
  sugar
200 g ($6^1/2$ oz) unsalted butter
1 tablespoon golden syrup
100 g ($3^1/3$ oz) dark chocolate,
  chopped
2 eggs, lightly beaten
cocoa powder, for dusting
icing sugar, for dusting

➤ PREHEAT OVEN to warm 160°C (315°F/Gas 2–3). Brush a deep 20 cm (8 inch) round cake tin with melted butter or oil.

1 Line base and sides of tin with baking paper. Combine water, rum and raisins in a small bowl; set aside. Sift the flours and cocoa in a large bowl; make a well in the centre.

2 Combine sugars, butter, syrup and chocolate in a medium pan. Stir over low heat until the butter and chocolate have melted and sugar has dissolved; remove from heat. Stir in raisins, water and rum.

3 Using a metal spoon, stir butter mixture into dry ingredients until combined. Add eggs; mix well until smooth. Pour mixture into prepared

tin; smooth surface. Bake 1–$1^1/4$ hours or until skewer comes out clean when inserted in centre of cake. Leave cake in tin 1 hour before turning onto wire rack to cool. Dust with combined sifted cocoa and icing sugar before serving. Serve warm with thick cream. Cake is best eaten on day it is made.

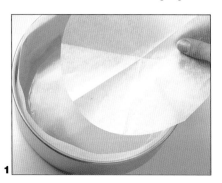

RICH MARBLED CHOCOLATE CAKE

Preparation time: 35 minutes
Total cooking time: 40 minutes
Makes one 20 cm (8 inch) round cake

125 g (4 oz) dark chocolate,
　chopped
125 g (4 oz) butter
$^1/_2$ cup (125 g/4 oz) caster sugar
2 eggs, lightly beaten
$1^1/_4$ cups (155 g/5 oz) self-
　raising flour
$^1/_3$ cup (80 ml/$2^3/_4$ fl oz) milk
1 tablespoon brandy
$^1/_2$ teaspoon vanilla essence

Chocolate Icing
100 g ($3^1/_3$ oz) white chocolate,
　chopped
4 tablespoons cream
100 g ($3^1/_3$ oz) dark chocolate,
　extra, chopped

► PREHEAT OVEN to moderate 180°C (350°F/Gas 4). Brush a deep 20 cm (8 inch) round cake tin with melted butter or oil. Line base and sides with baking paper. Place chocolate in heatproof bowl; stand bowl over a pan of simmering water. Stir until melted; remove from heat.

1 Using electric beaters, beat butter and sugar in a bowl until light and creamy. Add eggs gradually, beating thoroughly after each addition.

2 Transfer mixture to bowl. Using a metal spoon, fold in sifted flour alternately with milk. Add brandy and essence; stir until combined. Divide mixture in two; add melted chocolate to one portion and mix well.

3 Spoon the two mixtures alternately into prepared tin. Swirl mixture with skewer. Bake 40 minutes or until skewer comes out clean when inserted in centre. Leave cake in tin 15 minutes before turning onto wire rack to cool.

4 To make Chocolate Icing: Place white chocolate and 2 tablespoons cream in a small heatproof bowl; stand bowl over a pan of simmering water, stir until smooth. Repeat melting process with extra dark chocolate and remaining cream. Place alternate blobs of mixtures on top of cake. Swirl with a skewer for a marbled look. Cake is best eaten on day it is made.

1

2

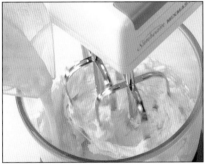

3

4

MOCHA RUM TORTE

Preparation time: 35 minutes
Total cooking time: 35 minutes
Makes one 20 cm (8 inch) cake

4 eggs
1/2 cup (125 g/4 oz) caster sugar
125 g (4 oz) dark chocolate,
    roughly chopped
1/3 cup (80 ml/2³/4 fl oz) strong
    black coffee
3/4 cup (90 g/3 oz) self-raising
    flour, sifted
2 tablespoons dark rum
1 tablespoon hot water
1 teaspoon sugar
1¹/2 cups (375 ml/12 fl oz)
    cream, whipped
dark chocolate, for shaving
1/2 cup (50 g/1²/3 oz) walnuts,
    chopped
icing sugar, for dusting

➤ PREHEAT OVEN to moderate 180°C (350°F/Gas 4). Brush two 20 cm (8 inch) shallow round cake tins with melted butter or oil. Line base and sides with baking paper.

1 Warm a large bowl by filling it with very hot water. Stand 1 minute; drain water and dry bowl thoroughly. Add eggs and sugar to warmed bowl. Using electric beaters, beat eggs and sugar for 5 minutes or until thick and pale in colour. Place chocolate in a small bowl; stand the bowl over a pan of simmering water; stir until the chocolate has melted. Stir in coffee and remove from heat.

2 Using a metal spoon, fold half the flour into egg mixture alternately with half the melted chocolate. Fold in remaining flour and chocolate; stir until mixture is smooth. Spoon mixture into prepared tins; smooth surface. Bake 30 minutes or until

skewer comes out clean when inserted in centre of each cake. Leave cakes in tins 10 minutes before turning onto wire racks to cool. Combine rum with hot water and sugar in a small bowl. Brush warm rum mixture over warm cakes. Cool completely.

3 *To assemble cake:* Place one cake

on serving plate; spread this cake evenly with one-third of the whipped cream. Place other cake on top. Spread top and sides with remaining cream. Decorate with shaved chocolate and walnuts. Dust with sifted icing sugar before serving. This cake is best eaten on the day it is made.

1

2

3

CHOCOLATE WALNUT RING

Preparation time: 35 minutes
Total cooking time: 35 minutes
Makes one 23 cm (9 inch) ring cake

$1^3/4$ cups (215 g/$6^3/4$ oz) self-
   raising flour
1 teaspoon bicarbonate of soda
$^1/2$ cup (60 g/2 oz) cocoa powder
$^3/4$ cup (185 g/6 oz) caster sugar
$^1/4$ cup (45 g/$1^1/2$ oz) soft
   brown sugar
1 teaspoon vanilla essence
2 eggs
1 cup (250 ml/8 fl oz) buttermilk
$^1/2$ cup (125 ml/4 fl oz) milk
60 g (2 oz) unsalted butter,
   melted
$^1/3$ cup (35 g/$1^1/4$ oz) walnuts,
   chopped

Chocolate Sauce
100 g ($3^1/3$ oz) dark chocolate,
   chopped
$^1/3$ cup (80 ml/$2^3/4$ fl oz) cream

▶PREHEAT OVEN to moderate
180°C (350°F/Gas 4). Brush a deep
23 cm (9 inch) fluted ring tin with
melted butter or oil.
1 Sift the flour, soda and cocoa into a
large bowl; add the sugars. Make a
well in the centre.
2 Add combined vanilla essence,
eggs, milks and butter to dry ingredients. Using electric beaters, beat mixture on low 3 minutes or until moist.
3 Beat mixture on high 5 minutes or
until smooth and increased in volume.
Fold in walnuts. Pour mixture into
prepared tin; smooth surface. Bake
35 minutes or until skewer comes out
clean when inserted in the centre of
the cake. Leave cake in tin 10 minutes;
turn onto a wire rack to cool.
4 To make Chocolate Sauce:
Combine chocolate and cream in small
pan. Stir over low heat until chocolate
melts and mixture is smooth. Remove
from heat; cool to room temperature.
Pour sauce over cake. Decorate with
two-toned chocolate curls and icing
sugar, if desired. May be served warm
as a dessert with thick cream or ice-
cream. This cake is best eaten on the
day it is made.

PEANUT AND CHOC CHIP MUFFIN CAKES

Preparation time: 15 minutes
Total cooking time: 20–25 minutes
Makes 12

2 cups (250 g/8 oz) self-raising
　flour
1/3 cup (80 g/2²/3 oz) raw sugar
1¹/2 cups (265 g/8¹/2 oz) dark
　choc bits
1 egg
1 cup (250 g/8 oz) crunchy
　peanut butter

2 tablespoons strawberry
　jam
60 g (2 oz) butter, melted
3/4 cup (185 ml/6 fl oz) milk
icing sugar, for dusting

➤ PREHEAT OVEN to moderate
180°C (350°F/Gas 4). Brush a 12-cup
(¹/2-cup capacity) muffin pan with
melted butter or oil.

1 Sift flour into a large bowl. Add
sugar and choc bits; make a well in
the centre. Add combined egg, peanut
butter, jam, butter and milk. Stir until
just combined (do not overbeat). If
you find the mixture is too dry, add

1/4 cup (60 ml/2 fl oz) milk, extra.
2 Spoon mixture evenly into muffin
cups. Bake 20–25 minutes or until
skewer comes out clean when inserted
in centre of cakes.
3 Loosen muffins in pan, leave
10 minutes before turning onto wire
rack to cool. Dust with icing sugar.

COOK'S FILE

Storage time: Peanut and Choc Chip
Muffins are best eaten warm when
straight out of the oven.
Hint: Use smooth peanut butter
instead of crunchy if muffins prove
too chunky.

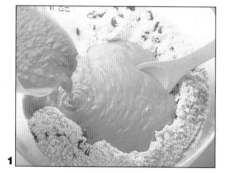

1

2

3

FLOURLESS CHOCOLATE NUT AND FRUIT CAKE

Preparation time: 30 minutes
Total cooking time: 1 hour
Makes one 24 cm (9¹/2 inch) round
　cake

100 g (3¹/3 oz) glacé apricots,
100 g (3¹/3 oz) glacé figs
80 g (2²/3 oz) glacé ginger
5 egg whites
3/4 cup (185 g/6 oz) caster sugar
250 g (8 oz) blanched almonds,
　finely chopped
250 g (8 oz) dark chocolate,
　chopped

60 g (2 oz) dark cooking
　chocolate, melted
1¹/2 cups (375 ml/12 fl oz) cream

➤ PREHEAT OVEN to slow 150°C
(300°F/Gas 2). Brush a deep 24 cm
(9¹/2 inch) round springform tin with
melted butter or oil. Line base and
sides with baking paper.
1 Chop the glacé fruit and ginger.
Using electric beaters, beat egg whites
until soft peaks form. Gradually add
sugar, beating well after each addition;
beat until sugar has dissolved and
mixture is thick and glossy.
2 Using a metal spoon, fold in fruit,
almonds and both chopped and melted chocolate. Stir until just combined.

Spread mixture in prepared tin; bake
1 hour or until skewer comes out clean
when inserted in the centre. Leave
cake in tin 15 minutes then cool on
wire rack.
3 When cake is completely cooled,
whip cream until stiff peaks form.
Using a piping bag fitted with a plain
nozzle, pipe swirls of cream on top of
cake. Decorate with chocolate leaves,
if desired (see page 7).

COOK'S FILE

Storage time: Keep cake (without
whipped cream topping) for up to
2 weeks in an airtight container. Pipe
with cream just before serving, or
dust with icing sugar if preferred.

1

2

3

Peanut and Choc Chip Muffin Cakes (top) and
Flourless Chocolate Nut and Fruit Cake

CHOCOLATE YOGHURT CAKE

Preparation time: 35 minutes
Total cooking time: 45 minutes
Makes one 23 cm (9 inch) round cake

1 cup (125 g/4 oz) self-raising
   flour
1/3 cup (40 g/1 1/3 oz) plain flour
1/4 cup (30 g/1 oz) cocoa powder
125 g (4 oz) butter
1 1/4 cups (310 g/9 3/4 oz) caster
   sugar
2 eggs, lightly beaten
1/2 cup (125 g/4 oz) plain
   yoghurt
1/2 cup (125 ml/4 fl oz) water
1 cup (250 ml/8 fl oz) cream,
   whipped

Topping
175 g (5 2/3 oz) white chocolate,
   roughly chopped
1/4 cup (60 ml/2 fl oz) cream
60 g (2 oz) dark chocolate,
   melted

➤ PREHEAT OVEN to moderate 180°C (350°F/Gas 4). Brush a deep 23 cm (9 inch) round cake tin with melted butter or oil. Line the base and sides with baking paper.

1 Sift flours and cocoa onto a sheet of baking paper. Using electric beaters, beat butter and sugar in large bowl until light and creamy. Add the eggs gradually, beating thoroughly after each addition. Combine yoghurt and water in small bowl.

2 Using a metal spoon, fold in sifted flours and cocoa alternately with yoghurt mixture. Stir until combined and mixture is smooth. Spoon the mixture into prepared tin; smooth surface. Bake for 45 minutes or until a skewer comes out clean when inserted in centre of cake. Leave cake in tin 10 minutes; turn onto wire rack to cool.

3 To make Topping: Combine white chocolate and cream in a small heatproof bowl; stand the bowl over a pan of simmering water. Stir until chocolate has melted and mixture is smooth. Cool slightly.

To assemble cake: Cut cake in half horizontally. Spread whipped cream over one half of cake; top with other half. Spread white chocolate mixture gently over top of cake. Place dark chocolate in small paper piping bag; seal end, snip off tip. Pipe fine rings of dark chocolate over white topping. Slowly drag a skewer from the centre of cake towards the edge. Clean the skewer and draw more regular lines through the rings to create a feathered pattern. Chocolate Yoghurt Cake is best eaten on the day it is made.

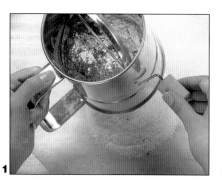

1

2

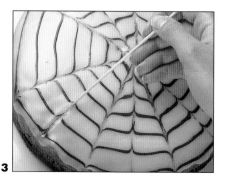

3

APRICOT SACHER CAKE

Preparation time: 45 minutes
Total cooking time: 50 minutes
Makes one 20 cm (8 inch) round cake

1 cup (125 g/4 oz) plain flour
1/2 cup (60 g/2 oz) cocoa powder
1/4 cup (80 g/2²/3 oz) apricot jam
1 cup (250 g/8 oz) caster sugar
125 g (4 oz) butter
4 eggs, separated
1/2 cup (160 g/5¹/4 oz) apricot
    jam, extra, heated

Ganache Topping
125 g (4 oz) dark cooking
    chocolate, chopped
1/2 cup (125 ml/4 fl oz) thick
    cream

➤ PREHEAT OVEN to moderate 180°C (350°F/Gas 4). Brush a deep 20 cm (8 inch) round cake tin with melted butter or oil. Line base and sides with baking paper.

1 Sift flour and cocoa into bowl. Make a well in the centre. Combine jam, sugar and butter in small pan; stir over low heat until sugar has dissolved and mixture is smooth. Remove from heat; cool slightly. Stir the butter mixture into flour until combined. Add egg yolks, mix well.

2 Place egg whites in small clean bowl. Using electric beaters, beat until soft peaks form. Using a metal spoon, fold whites into cake mixture. Pour into prepared tin. Bake 50 minutes or until skewer comes out clean when inserted in the centre. Leave cake in tin 15 minutes; turn onto wire rack to cool.

3 *To assemble cake:* Place cake upside-down on board. Cut cake horizontally into 3 even layers. Brush each layer with one-fifth of the jam; re-assemble cake and transfer to wire rack. Brush cake with remaining jam.

4 To make Ganache Topping: Combine chocolate and cream in small pan. Stir over low heat until melted and smooth. Cool until ganache has thickened slightly. Pour Ganache Topping completely over the cake. Smooth top and sides with a palette knife. Allow to set before transferring to serving plate. Decorate cake with large shavings of chocolate and dust with icing sugar and cocoa, if desired.

COOK'S FILE

Storage time: May be stored for up to two days in an airtight container.

COCONUT ROUGH CAKE

Preparation time: 30 minutes
Total cooking time: 50–55 minutes
Makes one 20 cm (8 inch) round cake

125 g (4 oz) butter
1/3 cup (90 g/3 oz) caster sugar
2 tablespoons demerara sugar
2 tablespoons golden syrup
2 eggs, lightly beaten
1/2 cup (45 g/1 1/2 oz) desiccated
    coconut
60 g (2 oz) dark chocolate,
    grated
1 1/2 cups (185 g/6 oz) self-
    raising flour
2/3 cup (170 ml/5 1/2 fl oz) milk
toasted flaked coconut, for
    decoration
icing sugar, for dusting

Icing
200 g (6 1/2 oz) milk chocolate,
    chopped
1/3 cup (90 g/3 oz) sour cream

➤ PREHEAT OVEN to moderate 180°C (350°F/Gas 4). Brush a deep 20 cm (8 inch) round cake tin with melted butter or oil. Line base and sides with baking paper.

1 Using electric beaters, beat butter and sugars in small bowl until light and creamy. Add golden syrup; beat thoroughly. Add the eggs gradually, beating well after each addition.

2 Transfer mixture to a large bowl; add coconut and chocolate. Using a metal spoon fold in sifted flour alternately with milk. Stir until the mixture is smooth. Spoon mixture into prepared tin; smooth surface. Bake 50–55 minutes or until skewer comes out clean when inserted in the centre. Leave cake in tin 10 minutes before turning onto wire rack to cool.

3 To make Icing: Combine the chocolate and sour cream in a small pan. Stir over low heat until chocolate has melted and mixture is smooth; remove from heat. Cool. Spread a thin layer of icing over top of cake. Spoon remaining icing into an icing bag fitted with a fluted nozzle. Pipe swirls around inner edge of cake. Decorate with flaked coconut. Dust with icing sugar. If preferred, leave off icing and top with freshly whipped cream.

CHOCOLATE CREAM CUPS

Preparation time: 30 minutes
Total cooking time: 30–35 minutes
Makes about 30

1 cup (125 g/4 oz) self-raising
   flour
$^{1}/_{4}$ cup (30 g/1 oz) plain flour
$^{1}/_{4}$ cup (30 g/1 oz) cocoa powder
$^{1}/_{2}$ teaspoon bicarbonate
   of soda
180 g ($5^{3}/_{4}$ oz) dark chocolate,
   chopped
150 g ($4^{3}/_{4}$ oz) butter
$^{1}/_{2}$ cup (90 g/$3^{1}/_{4}$ oz) soft
   brown sugar
$^{1}/_{4}$ cup (60 ml/2 fl oz) water
$^{1}/_{4}$ cup (60 ml/2 fl oz) buttermilk
1 egg, lightly beaten
60 g (2 oz) dark compound
   chocolate, melted
$^{1}/_{2}$ cup (125 ml/4 fl oz) thick
   cream or 1 cup (250 ml/
   8 fl oz) cream, whipped
30 g (1 oz) butter

➤ PREHEAT OVEN to moderate 180°C (350°F/Gas 4). Line two 12-cup deep patty tins with paper cases.

1 Sift flours, cocoa and soda into a large bowl. Make a well in the centre. Combine 100 g ($3^{1}/_{3}$ oz) chocolate, butter, sugar and water in medium pan. Stir over low heat until ingredients have melted and mixture is smooth.

2 Gradually add chocolate mixture, buttermilk and egg to dry ingredients. Using a metal spoon, stir until the mixture is smooth. Spoon mixture into each patty case to about two-thirds full. Bake 30–35 minutes or until skewer comes out clean when inserted into centre of cakes. Transfer to wire rack to cool. Repeat process with remaining patty cases and mixture.

3 When patty cakes are cold, cut a small cavity in the top of each one, to a depth of about 1 cm ($^{1}/_{2}$ inch). Melt remaining 80 g ($2^{2}/_{3}$ oz) chocolate and butter together. Stir until smooth; cool slightly. Spoon a small amount of chocolate filling in top of each cake. Place melted compound chocolate in a small paper piping bag; seal end and snip off tip. Pipe small shapes onto sheets of baking paper; allow to set. Spoon or pipe cream onto the cakes; decorate with the chocolate shapes.

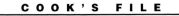

COOK'S FILE

Storage time: Cakes can be made up to two days ahead. Fill and decorate just before serving.
Hint: Crumble discarded cake tops to and use in rum balls or truffles. (See Petits Fours chapter in this book.)

COFFEE AND CHOCOLATE ROULADE

Preparation time: 40 minutes
Total cooking time: 10–15 minutes
Makes one large roll

6 eggs, separated
$^{3}/_{4}$ cup (185 g/6 oz) caster sugar
$^{2}/_{3}$ cup (85 g/2$^{3}/_{4}$ oz) self-raising flour
$^{1}/_{2}$ teaspoon ground cinnamon
$^{1}/_{2}$ teaspoon mixed spice
2 teaspoons instant coffee powder
$^{1}/_{3}$ cup (40 g/1$^{1}/_{3}$ oz) cocoa powder
50 g (1$^{2}/_{3}$ oz) dark chocolate, grated

Coffee Buttercream
$^{1}/_{3}$ cup (80 ml/2$^{3}/_{4}$ fl oz) cream
150 g (4$^{3}/_{4}$ oz) white chocolate melts
200 g (6$^{1}/_{2}$ oz) butter
$^{3}/_{4}$ cup (90 g/3 oz) icing sugar
1 teaspoon vanilla essence
1–2 tablespoons coffee or chocolate liqueur
2 teaspoons instant coffee powder

➤ PREHEAT OVEN to moderate 180°C (350°F/Gas 4).
1 Brush two 30 x 25 x 2 cm (12 x 19 x $^{3}/_{4}$ inch) shallow Swiss roll tins with melted butter or oil. Line base and sides with baking paper. Beat egg whites with electric beaters until soft peaks form. Slowly add a third of the sugar; beat well until sugar has dissolved and mixture is thick and glossy.
2 In a separate bowl, beat egg yolks and remaining sugar until thick, pale and creamy. Using a metal spoon, gradually fold in egg white mixture alternately with combined sifted flour,

spices, coffee and cocoa, and grated chocolate. Stir gently until smooth. Spread mixture evenly into prepared tins. Bake 10–15 minutes or until cooked through and cake springs back when lightly touched. Cover two tea-towels with greaseproof paper and sprinkle with caster sugar. Turn cakes out onto paper; leave for 1 minute.
3 Peel baking paper from cakes and discard. Using the tea-towel as a guide, roll up cakes and paper from the long side. Roll one cake tighter than the other. Leave cakes 5 minutes or until almost cool, then unroll.
4 To make Coffee Buttercream: Heat cream in a small pan until almost boiling. Remove from heat and add chocolate. Stand 1–2 minutes; stir until smooth. Set aside to cool.
5 Using electric beaters, beat butter until light and creamy. Gradually add sifted icing sugar; continue beating until well combined. Add combined essence, liqueur and coffee; mix well. Gradually beat in chocolate mixture; beat until thick and creamy.
6 Divide Buttercream into three. Spread two-thirds of the mixture on cakes. Trim edges of cakes with a sharp knife so that they are an exact fit. Starting with more tightly rolled cake, roll up cakes from the long side and press together firmly. Wrap tightly with plastic wrap and refrigerate for 15 minutes. Spread Roulade with remaining Buttercream. Trim ends with sharp knife. Decorate top with dark and white chocolate curls and dust with icing sugar, if desired.

COOK'S FILE

Storage time: Cake can be made up to three days in advance.
Variation: Omit coffee and liqueur in Buttercream and add 1–2 teaspoons of grated orange or lemon rind and 1–2 tablespoons of lemon or orange juice.

1

2

3

4

5

6

LAYERED BERRY AND CHOCOLATE CREAM CAKE

Preparation time: 30 minutes
Total cooking time: 40–45 minutes
Makes one 20 cm (8 inch) round cake

125 g (4 oz) cream cheese
60 g (2 oz) butter
³/₄ cup (185 g/6 oz) caster sugar
2 eggs, lightly beaten
100 g (3¹/₃ oz) dark chocolate, melted
2 cups (250 g/8 oz) plain flour
¹/₄ cup (30 g/1 oz) cocoa powder
1 teaspoon bicarbonate of soda
³/₄ cup (185 ml/6 fl oz) water
strawberries, raspberries or young berries, for decoration

White Chocolate Cream
125 g (4 oz) white chocolate melts
¹/₄ cup (60 ml/2 fl oz) cream

Filling
2 cups (500 ml/16 fl oz) cream, whipped
250 g (8 oz) strawberries or raspberries, quartered

▶ PREHEAT OVEN to moderate 180°C (350°F/Gas 4). Brush a deep 20 cm (8 inch) round cake tin with melted butter or oil. Line base and sides with baking paper.

1 Using electric beaters, beat cream cheese, butter and sugar in small bowl until light and creamy. Add eggs gradually, beating thoroughly after each addition. Add chocolate; beat until smooth.

2 Transfer mixture to a large bowl. Using a metal spoon, fold in sifted flour, cocoa and soda alternately with water. Stir until combined and mixture is smooth. Pour mixture evenly into prepared tin; smooth surface. Bake 45–50 minutes or until skewer comes out clean when inserted in the centre. Stand cake in tin 5–10 minutes before turning onto wire rack to cool.

3 To make White Chocolate Cream: Combine chocolate and cream in a small heatproof bowl. Stand bowl over a pan of simmering water; stir until chocolate has melted and mixture is smooth. Cool in refrigerator until spreadable, stirring occasionally.
To assemble cake: Cut the cake horizontally into three even layers. Place base layer on serving plate. Spread base with White Chocolate Cream; top with one-fifth of the whipped cream, then half of the berries. Top with second layer of cake and repeat layering with remaining Chocolate Cream, a quarter of the cream and remaining berries. Top with last layer of cake. Spread cake sides and top evenly with remaining cream. Decorate cake with berries. Basic cake can be made several days ahead. Store in the refrigerator.

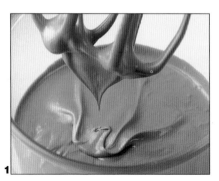

CHOCOLATE CHERRY CAKE

Preparation time: 20 minutes
Total cooking time: 1 hour
Makes one 23 cm (9 inch) round cake

670 g (1 lb 5²/₃ oz) bottled pitted morello cherries
3 eggs
1 cup (250 g/8 oz) caster sugar
2 teaspoons grated lemon rind
125 g (4 oz) softened butter
¹/₄ cup (60 ml/2 fl oz) vegetable oil

125 g (4 oz) dark chocolate, melted
2²/₃ cups (335 g/10¹/₂ oz) self-raising flour
200 g (6¹/₂ oz) plain yoghurt
1 cup (175 g/5²/₃ oz) dark choc bits
icing sugar and cocoa powder, for dusting

➤ PREHEAT OVEN to moderate 180°C (350°F/Gas 4). Brush a deep 23 cm (9 inch) round cake tin with melted butter. Line base and sides with baking paper. Drain cherries reserving 2 tablespoons syrup.

1 Using electric beaters, beat eggs and sugar in bowl until combined. Add rind, butter and oil; beat until mixture is smooth. Beat in chocolate. Transfer cake mixture to a large bowl.
2 Add sifted flour, yoghurt and reserved syrup. Using a metal spoon, fold in drained cherries and choc bits.
3 Spread mixture into prepared tin; smooth surface. Bake 1 hour or until skewer comes out clean when inserted in centre. Leave cake in tin 5 minutes before turning onto wire rack to cool. Dust all over with sifted icing sugar; dust a smaller ring of cocoa over the top. Serve with thick cream, if desired.

ORANGE CHOCOLATE MUD CAKE

Preparation time: 35 minutes +
  20 minutes standing
Total cooking time: 1 hour
Makes one 23 cm (9 inch) round cake

$^3/_4$ cup (140 g/4$^2/_3$ oz) mixed
  peel
350 g (11$^1/_4$ oz) dark cooking
  chocolate, chopped
225 g (7$^1/_4$ oz) butter
$^1/_3$ cup (80 ml/2$^3/_4$ fl oz) warm
  water
$^2/_3$ cup (85 g/2$^3/_4$ oz) plain flour
1$^1/_4$ cups (230 g/7$^1/_3$ oz) ground
  almonds
5 eggs, separated
1$^1/_4$ cups (310 g/9$^3/_4$ oz) caster
  sugar
1 tablespoon Cointreau liqueur
mixed peel, extra, for decoration

Chocolate Butter
200 g (6$^1/_2$ oz) butter
200 g (6$^1/_2$ oz) dark chocolate,
chopped

► PREHEAT OVEN to moderate 180°C (350°F/Gas 4). Brush a deep 23 cm (9 inch) round cake tin with melted butter or oil. Line base and sides with baking paper. Process mixed peel until very fine.

1 Melt chocolate and butter in medium pan over low heat. Stir in warm water. Remove from heat; cool slightly.

2 Combine flour and almonds in bowl. Using electric beaters, beat yolks and sugar in a large bowl until thick and pale yellow in colour. Using a metal spoon, stir in chocolate mixture; mix until combined. Fold in combined flour and almonds, processed peel and liqueur. In a separate bowl, beat egg whites with electric beaters until soft peaks form; fold into mixture. Spread mixture into prepared tin; smooth surface. Bake 1 hour or until skewer comes out clean when inserted in the centre. Leave in tin 20 minutes; turn onto a wire rack to cool.

3 To make Chocolate Butter: Combine butter and chocolate in a medium pan. Stir over low heat until chocolate has melted and mixture is smooth. Cool, stirring occasionally, until mixture becomes spreadable.

4 Spread top of cooled cake with one-third of the Chocolate Butter. Place remaining chocolate butter in piping bag fitted with a fluted nozzle. Pipe rosettes around the outer edge of cake. Decorate with extra mixed peel.

CHOCOLATE SWISS ROLL WITH STRAWBERRIES

Preparation time: 30 minutes
Total cooking time: 12 minutes
Serves 6–8

icing sugar, for dusting
3 eggs
$1/2$ cup (125 g/4 oz) caster sugar
150 g ($4^3/4$ oz) dark chocolate, finely grated
$1/2$ cup (95 g/$3^1/4$ oz) ground almonds
$1/2$ cup (60 g/2 oz) plain flour

Filling
150 g ($4^3/4$ oz) dark cooking chocolate, chopped

1 tablespoon water
$1^1/4$ cups (315 ml/10 fl oz) cream, whipped
250 g (8 oz) strawberries, quartered
whipped cream, extra
strawberries, extra

➤ PREHEAT OVEN to hot 210°C (415°F/Gas 6–7). Brush a 25 x 30 x 2 cm (10 x 12 x $3/4$ inch) shallow Swiss roll tin with melted butter or oil. Line base and sides with baking paper. Lay a sheet of baking paper on a clean tea-towel; sprinkle paper heavily with sifted icing sugar.

1 Using electric beaters, beat eggs and sugar in medium bowl 5 minutes or until thick and creamy. Using a metal spoon, fold in grated chocolate, almonds and sifted flour. Spread mixture into prepared tin. Bake 12 minutes or until just firm when touched in centre.

2 Quickly turn cake onto icing-sugar paper. Remove tin and baking paper from cake; cool 2 minutes, then roll cake from short side, using paper as a guide. Set aside the rolled cake for 10 minutes. Unroll carefully and cool.

3 To make Filling: Melt chocolate and water together. Stir until smooth; cool. Spread mixture on cake. Top with cream and strawberries, leaving a 2 cm ($3/4$ inch) border around the edge. Roll cake into a log shape. Pipe swirls of cream on top. Decorate with strawberries and white chocolate curls. Dust with cocoa powder if desired. This cake is best eaten on the day it is made.

1

2

3

BISCUITS & SLICES

CHOCOLATE HAZELNUT ROUNDS

Preparation time: 50 minutes
Total cooking time: 15–20 minutes
Makes 48

60 g (2 oz) roasted hazelnuts
60 g (2 oz) dark chocolate,
    finely chopped
125 g (4 oz) butter
$^1/_2$ cup (125 g/4 oz) caster sugar
1 egg
1 cup (125 g/4 oz) plain flour
$^1/_4$ cup (30 g/1 oz) self-raising
    flour
$^1/_2$ teaspoon ground cardamom
125 g (4 oz) white chocolate,
    roughly chopped
48 roasted hazelnuts, extra
80 g ($2^2/_3$ oz) dark chocolate,
    extra, melted

➤ PREHEAT OVEN to moderate 180°C (350°F/Gas 4). Brush two oven trays with melted butter or oil. Line with baking paper.
1 Place hazelnuts and chocolate in food processor; using pulse action, process in short bursts until just finely ground. (The mixture will be sticky if over-processed.) Using electric beaters, beat butter and sugar in a large bowl until light and creamy. Add egg and beat well. Add combined sifted flours and cardamom; stir with a knife to mix well. Add chocolate and nut mixture and mix to form a soft dough.
2 Roll 2 level teaspoons of mixture into a ball and place on prepared trays, allowing room for spreading. Flatten balls slightly with fingers. Bake for 15 minutes or until golden brown. Transfer to wire rack to cool.
3 Place white chocolate in a small heatproof bowl. Stand bowl over a pan of simmering water. Stir until chocolate has melted and mixture is smooth. Remove from heat. Dip the biscuits halfway in white chocolate and return to wire rack for chocolate to set. Dip extra hazelnuts into the melted dark chocolate; drain off excess. Place a chocolate coated hazelnut in the centre of each biscuit. Allow chocolate to set.

COOK'S FILE

Storage time: Biscuits will keep up to four days in an airtight container.
Variations: Alternate chocolate colours using combinations of white, milk and dark chocolate; dip half of each biscuit in white chocolate and the other half in milk chocolate. Place a dark chocolate nut on top.

2

3

CRISPY CHOCOLATE MERINGUES

Preparation time: 20 minutes
Total cooking time: 25–30 minutes
Makes 30

2 egg whites
1/2 cup (125 g/4 oz) caster sugar
1 1/4 cups (35 g/1 1/4 oz)
    cornflakes, crushed
125 g (4 oz) dark chocolate,
    finely chopped
2 tablespoons drinking
    chocolate, for dusting

►PREHEAT OVEN to warm 160°C (315°F/Gas 2–3). Brush an oven tray with melted butter or oil. Line with baking paper; grease paper.

1 Using electric beaters, beat egg whites in small bowl until stiff peaks form. Add sugar gradually and beat until sugar has dissolved and mixture is thick and glossy.

2 Using a metal spoon, fold the cornflakes and chocolate gently into the egg white mixture and stir until well combined.

3 Spoon 2 heaped teaspoons of the meringue mixture on prepared baking tray 2 cm (3/4 inch) apart. Bake 25–30 minutes or until dry and firm to touch. Dust meringues with sifted drinking chocolate while still hot. Transfer to a wire rack when almost cool.

COOK'S FILE

Storage time: Store meringues for up to a week in an airtight container.

Meringues can be frozen for up to 6 months. Thaw slowly in the refrigerator, leaving them wrapped or still in their container so that no moisture gets in. If meringues need re-crisping, heat oven, turn it off and place the meringues, uncovered, in oven for several minutes.

1

2

3

SULTANA AND CHOCOLATE CORNFLAKE COOKIES

Preparation time: 30 minutes
Total cooking time: 15 minutes
Makes 40

1 teaspoon grated orange rind
$^1/_3$ cup (60 g/2 oz) dark choc bits
$^1/_2$ cup (60 g/2 oz) sultanas
$^1/_4$ cup (25 g/$^3/_4$ oz) walnuts, roughly chopped
125 g (4 oz) butter, chopped

$^1/_3$ cup (90 g/3 oz) caster sugar
1 egg
1 cup (125 g/4 oz) self-raising flour, sifted
2$^1/_4$ cups (65 g/2$^1/_4$ oz) cornflakes, lightly crushed
80 g (2$^2/_3$ oz) dark chocolate, melted

► PREHEAT OVEN to moderate 180°C (350°F/Gas 4). Brush two oven trays with melted butter or oil.

1 Combine the orange rind, choc bits, sultanas and walnuts in medium bowl.
2 Using electric beaters, beat butter and sugar in small bowl until light and creamy. Add egg and beat well. Transfer mixture to large bowl. Using a metal spoon, fold in flour. Add the sultana mixture and stir to combine.
3 Roll 2 level teaspoons of mixture in crushed cornflakes to coat. Place on prepared tray and bake 15 minutes or until golden and crisp. Transfer to wire rack to cool. Pipe or drizzle melted chocolate over cooled biscuits.

COOK'S FILE

Storage time: Keep up to a week in an airtight container.
Hint: Use currants or chopped raisins in place of sultanas.

1

2

3

CRUNCHY CHOCOLATE BARS

Preparation time: 30 minutes
Total cooking time: 5–10 minutes
Makes 30

1/3 cup (60 g/2 oz) soft brown
   sugar
1/3 cup (80 ml/2³/4 fl oz) light
   corn syrup
30 g (1 oz) unsalted butter
1/4 cup (45 g/1¹/2 oz) dark choc
   bits

1/2 cup (120 g/4 oz) crunchy
   peanut butter
4 cups (125 g/4 oz) Rice Bubbles
60 g (2 oz) dark chocolate,
   chopped

▶BRUSH A 30 x 20 cm (12 x 8 inch) tin with melted butter or oil. Line base with baking paper extending over two sides; grease paper.

1 Place sugar and corn syrup in small pan and stir over low heat, without boiling, until sugar dissolves. Bring to boil; reduce heat. Add butter and choc bits; remove from heat. Stir until melted and smooth. Stir in peanut butter and mix well.

2 Place Rice Bubbles in medium bowl; add the warm chocolate mixture and stir to combine. (Work quickly before chocolate sets.) Pour mixture into prepared tin; press down firmly with lightly oiled hands. Allow to set.

3 Place chocolate in a small heatproof bowl over a pan of simmering water; stir until melted. Cool slightly. Place in small paper icing bag; seal end and snip off tip. Pipe a fine diagonal lattice pattern over mixture. Leave to set. Remove and cut into small bars.

COCONUT CHOCOLATE CHERRY TRIANGLES

Preparation time: 25–30 minutes +
    4 hours refrigeration
Total cooking time: 20 minutes
Makes 35

125 g (4 oz) dark chocolate,
    chopped
3 eggs
³/₄ cup (185 g/6 oz) caster sugar
60 g (2 oz) unsalted butter,
    melted

¹/₂ cup (105 g/3¹/₂ oz) glacé
    cherries, roughly chopped
2¹/₂ cups (225 g/7¹/₄ oz)
    desiccated coconut
icing sugar, for dusting

➤ PREHEAT OVEN to moderate 180°C (350°F/Gas 4). Brush a shallow 23 cm (9 inch) square cake tin with melted butter or oil. Line base with baking paper, extending over two sides; grease paper.

1 Place chocolate in medium heat-proof bowl; stand bowl over pan of simmering water and stir until the chocolate has melted. Pour chocolate into prepared tin and spread evenly with the back of a spoon. Allow to set.

2 Using electric beaters, beat eggs and sugar in a small mixing bowl until pale and creamy. Transfer to a large bowl; fold in butter, cherries and coconut. Pour over chocolate in the prepared tin; smooth surface.

3 Bake 15–20 minutes or until the top is golden. Cool, then refrigerate 4 hours or until chocolate has set. Remove from tin; peel away paper and cut into 6 cm (2 inch) triangles with a hot knife. Dust with icing sugar.

43

CHOCOLATE BISCUIT SHAPES

Preparation time: 35–40 minutes
Total cooking time: 25–30 minutes
Makes about 26

45 g (1¹/₂ oz) dark chocolate,
  roughly chopped
125 g (4 oz) unsalted butter,
  chopped
¹/₄ cup (30 g/1 oz) icing sugar
1 egg, lightly beaten
1¹/₂ cups (185 g/6 oz) plain
  flour
1 tablespoon cornflour
2 tablespoons cocoa powder
100 g (3¹/₃ oz) white chocolate

▶ PREHEAT OVEN to moderate 180°C (350°F/Gas 4). Brush two oven trays with melted butter or oil. Line with baking paper.

1 Place dark chocolate in small heat-proof bowl; stand bowl over pan of simmering water and stir until melted and smooth.

2 Using electric beaters, beat butter and sugar in small bowl until light and creamy; add egg, then melted chocolate. Beat well. Transfer mixture to a medium bowl. Add sifted flours and cocoa; mix with a knife until well combined.

3 Turn dough onto lightly floured surface; knead lightly for 30 seconds or until smooth. Roll between 2 sheets of greaseproof paper to 1 cm (¹/₂ inch) thickness. Cut out shapes with some assorted animal or decorative biscuit cutters. Place on prepared trays and bake for 20 minutes or until firm to touch. Remove and transfer to a wire rack to cool.

4 Roughly chop or grate chocolate and place in a small heatproof bowl; stand bowl over a pan of simmering water and stir until chocolate has melted and mixture is smooth. Remove from heat; cool slightly. Place white chocolate in a small paper icing bag. Seal and snip off the tip. Pipe decorations and fine lines of white chocolate around each biscuit.

COOK'S FILE

Storage time: Biscuit Shapes can be made up a week ahead. Store in an airtight container between sheets of greaseproof paper.

Variation: Pipe with dark chocolate instead of white, or dip the tops of the biscuits in melted chocolate.

Hints: These biscuits make a good inclusion in a presentation box of sweets. Use a selection of shapes and icing decorations.

Alternatively, wrap several animal biscuits in transparent cellophane, tie with a coloured ribbon and attach to the Christmas tree.

CHOC-NUT MARSHMALLOW TOPS

Preparation time: 35–40 minutes
Total cooking time: 12 minutes
Makes 50

155 g (5 oz) butter
60 g (2 oz) dark chocolate
¹/₃ cup (60 g/2 oz) soft brown sugar
1 egg
1¹/₄ cups (155 g/5 oz) plain flour
¹/₂ teaspoon bicarbonate of soda
¹/₄ cup (25 g/³/₄ oz) pecans, finely chopped
¹/₄ cup (25 g/³/₄ oz) walnuts, finely chopped
³/₄ cup (65 g/2¹/₄ oz) white marshmallows
30 g (1 oz) unsalted butter
¹/₂ cup (30 g/1 oz) shredded coconut, toasted

➤ PREHEAT OVEN to moderate 180°C (350°F/Gas 4). Brush two oven trays with melted butter or oil. Line tray with baking paper.

1 Cut butter into cubes. Using a large, sharp knife, roughly chop chocolate. Place chocolate in small heatproof bowl; stand bowl over pan of simmering water and stir until chocolate has melted and mixture is smooth. Remove from heat.

2 Using electric beaters, beat butter and sugar in small bowl until light and creamy. Add egg and beat well. Transfer mixture to a medium bowl. Stir in sifted flour and soda with a knife. Add melted chocolate and nuts and stir to combine. Place heaped teaspoons of mixture on prepared trays, allowing room for spreading. Bake 12 minutes or until firm to touch. Transfer biscuits to wire rack to cool.

3 Place marshmallows and unsalted butter in heatproof bowl; stand bowl over pan of simmering water. Stir until butter and marshmallows have melted and the mixture is smooth.

4 Place a teaspoon of marshmallow mixture on each biscuit; sprinkle with coconut. Allow to set before storing.

COOK'S FILE

Variation: Use coloured marshmallows instead of white.

CHOCOLATE NUT CREAMS

Preparation time: 1 hour
Total cooking time: 10–12 minutes per
  batch
Makes about 50

180 g (5³/4 oz) butter
¹/2 cup (125 g/4 oz) caster sugar
1 egg, lightly beaten
1 teaspoon grated orange rind
25 g (³/4 oz) dark chocolate,
  grated
1 tablespoon cocoa powder
1 cup (125 g/4 oz) self-raising
  flour
3³/4 cups (465 g/14¹/2 oz) plain
  flour
1–2 tablespoons milk
150 g (4³/4 oz) walnuts, toasted
  and finely chopped
100 g (3¹/3 oz) dark chocolate,
  chopped
100 g (3¹/3 oz) dark chocolate
  melts

Filling
180 g (5³/4 oz) butter
²/3 cup (85 g/2³/4 oz) icing
  sugar
4 teaspoons cocoa powder

► PREHEAT OVEN to moderate 180°C (350°F/Gas 4). Line two oven trays with baking paper.

1 Using electric beaters, beat butter and sugar until light and creamy. Add egg, rind and chocolate; beat until well combined. Transfer mixture to a large bowl. Using a flat-bladed knife, fold in sifted cocoa and flours and enough milk to form a soft dough. Turn onto lightly floured surface and knead 1–2 minutes or until smooth.

2 Divide dough in two. Roll each portion between two sheets of baking paper to 3–4 mm thickness. Cut into 5 cm (2 inch) rounds using a fluted biscuit cutter; place on prepared trays. Bake 10–12 minutes. Leave biscuits on trays 2 minutes, then transfer to wire rack to cool. Continue with remaining dough, re-rolling and re-using dough after cutting.

3 To make Filling: Beat butter and icing sugar with electric beaters until light and creamy. Add cocoa; beat a further 2 minutes or until smooth.

To assemble biscuits: Spread each biscuit with a small amount of filling (about 5 mm/¹/4 inch thick), leaving a 5 mm (¹/4 inch) border. Place chopped nuts in a small saucer. Dip tops of biscuits in nuts; shake off excess. Place biscuits on a tray and refrigerate 5–10 minutes. Place chocolate in heatproof bowl over a pan of simmering water. Stir until chocolate has melted. Remove from heat; cool slightly. Dip biscuits in melted chocolate, coating the filling and top of biscuit only; place on wire rack to set.

COOK'S FILE

Variation: Use a mixture of dried or glacé fruits for filling if preferred.

1

2

3

CHOC-FILLED SHORTBREADS

Preparation time: 50 minutes +
   45 minutes refrigeration
Total cooking time: 15–20 minutes
Makes 20

125 g (4 oz) butter, chopped
1/2 cup (60 g/2 oz) icing sugar
1 teaspoon grated orange rind
1 cup (125 g/4 oz) self-raising
   flour
1/2 cup (60 g/2 oz) cornflour
1 tablespoon iced water
1 tablespoon icing sugar, extra
1 tablespoon drinking chocolate

Filling
60 g (2 oz) dark chocolate,
   roughly chopped
60 g (2 oz) cream cheese
1 egg, lightly beaten

➤ PREHEAT OVEN to moderate 180°C (350°F/Gas 4). Brush two oven trays with melted butter or oil. Line with baking paper.

1 Using electric beaters, beat butter, icing sugar and orange rind until light and creamy. Transfer mixture to food processor and add sifted flours and water. Process for 20 seconds or until the mixture comes together. Wrap in plastic wrap and refrigerate 45 minutes.

2 To make Filling: Place chocolate in small heatproof bowl; stand bowl over pan of simmering water until chocolate has melted. Remove from heat. Using electric beaters, beat cream cheese until soft; add cooled chocolate and half of the beaten egg; mix well.

3 Roll out biscuit mixture between two sheets of greaseproof paper to a 3 mm (about 1/4 inch) thickness. Cut

into 5 cm (2 inch) rounds using a fluted cutter. Place 1/2 teaspoon of filling in the centre of half the rounds; brush edges with remaining beaten egg and place remaining rounds over filling. Press edges to seal. Place on prepared trays. Bake 10–15 minutes or until golden. Transfer to wire rack. Dust warm biscuits with combined sifted icing sugar and drinking chocolate.

COOK'S FILE

Storage time: Store in an airtight container for up to a week.

1

2

3

COCONUT CHOCOLATE SLICE

Preparation time: 40 minutes
Total cooking time: 30 minutes
Makes a 28 x 18 cm (11 x 7 inch) slice

$^1/_2$ cup (60 g/2 oz) plain flour
$^1/_2$ cup (60 g/2 oz) self-raising flour
2 tablespoons cocoa powder
$^2/_3$ cup (160 g/5$^1/_4$ oz) caster sugar
$^3/_4$ cup (65 g/2$^1/_4$ oz) desiccated coconut
125 g (4 oz) butter, melted
$^1/_2$ teaspoon vanilla essence

1 egg, lightly beaten
45 g (1$^1/_2$ oz) unsalted butter
90 g (3 oz) dark chocolate, roughly chopped
2 tablespoons cream

Topping
1 tablespoon lemon juice
$^1/_2$ cup (160 g/5$^1/_4$ oz) apricot jam

➤ PREHEAT OVEN to moderate 180°C (350°F/Gas 4). Brush a shallow 28 x 18 cm (11 x 7 inch) tin with melted butter. Line base with baking paper.

1 Sift flours and cocoa in medium bowl. Add sugar and coconut; make a well in the centre. Add butter, essence and egg; combine with a wooden spoon. Spoon the mixture into the prepared tin and smooth surface. Bake 20–25 minutes or until set. Leave to cool in tin.

2 To make Topping: Place lemon juice and jam in pan and stir over low heat. When bubbling, pour over slice; spread evenly with flat-bladed knife. Leave to set for 20 minutes.

3 Melt butter in small pan. Add chocolate and cream; remove from heat. Stir until chocolate melts and mixture is smooth. Spread over slice and leave to set. Cut slice into small squares. Decorate with chocolate curls, if desired. Store up to four days in an airtight container.

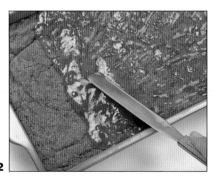

CHOCOLATE PEPPERMINT CREAMS

Preparation time: 40 minutes
Total cooking time: 10 minutes each
  tray
Makes about 30

65 g (2^1/$_4$ oz) unsalted butter
^{1}/$_4$ cup (60 g/2 oz) caster sugar
^{1}/$_2$ cup (60 g/2 oz) plain flour
^{1}/$_3$ cup (40 g/1^1/$_3$ oz) self-raising
  flour
2 tablespoons cocoa powder
2 tablespoons milk

Peppermint Cream
1 egg white
1^3/$_4$ cups (220 g/7 oz) icing
  sugar, sifted
2–3 drops peppermint essence
  or oil, to taste

Chocolate Topping
150 g (4^3/$_4$ oz) dark chocolate,
  chopped

➤ PREHEAT OVEN to moderate 180°C (350°F/Gas 4). Line two oven trays with baking paper.

1 Using electric beaters, beat butter and sugar in small bowl until light and creamy. Transfer to medium bowl. Add sifted flours and cocoa, alternately with the milk; mix with a knife until mixture forms a soft dough. Turn out onto a floured surface; knead 1 minute or until smooth.

2 Cut dough in half. Roll one half between two sheets of baking paper to 3 mm (^{1}/$_4$ inch) thickness. Cut dough into rounds using a 4 cm (1^1/$_2$ inch) plain biscuit cutter. Place on prepared trays, allowing room for spreading. Bake 10 minutes. Transfer to wire rack to cool completely. Repeat using

remaining dough. (The dough scraps can also be re-rolled.)

3 To make Peppermint Cream: Place egg white in small bowl. With electric beaters, beat in icing sugar, 2 tablespoons at a time, on low speed. Add more icing sugar, if necessary, until a soft dough forms.

4 Turn dough onto surface dusted with icing sugar; knead in enough icing sugar so that dough is not sticky. Knead in the peppermint essence, to taste.

5 Roll level teaspoons of peppermint cream into balls; flatten slightly. Sandwich between two chocolate biscuits, pressing together to spread peppermint to edges.

6 To make Chocolate Topping: Place chocolate in a small heatproof bowl; stand the bowl over a pan of simmering water. Stir until chocolate has melted and mixture is smooth. Remove from heat; cool slightly. Dip the biscuits halfway into the chocolate; drain away any excess chocolate. Stand on lined tray to allow topping to set. Serve with coffee or as after-dinner mints.

COOK'S FILE

Storage time: Store Chocolate Peppermint Creams in an airtight container in a cool place for up to 2 weeks.
Hints: Peppermint Cream can be adapted to make other biscuit creams by adding other essence flavourings. Add a few drops of appropriate food colouring if you like.

Leftover melted chocolate need not be discarded. Reserve in bowl (re-melt slightly, if necessary) and stir in chopped nuts, raisins, muesli or whatever you have to hand. Drop spoonfuls of the mixture onto grease-proof paper and leave to set. Plain sweet biscuits can also be dipped in leftover chocolate.

4

5

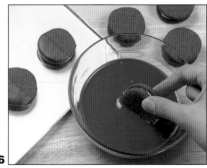

6

CHOC-CARROT SLICE

Preparation time: 20 minutes
Total cooking time: 40 minutes
Makes a 30 x 20 cm (12 x 8 inch) slice

1 cup (250 ml/8 fl oz) oil
3 eggs
1 cup (185 g/6 oz) soft brown
   sugar
1^3/$_4$ cups (215 g/6^3/$_4$ oz) self-
   raising flour, sifted
1 teaspoon bicarbonate of soda
2 teaspoons ground cinnamon
2 tablespoons cocoa powder

1 cup (130 g/4^1/$_4$ oz) grated
   dark chocolate
2 cups (310 g/9^3/$_4$ oz) grated
   carrot
^{1}/$_3$ cup (110 g/3^2/$_3$ oz) golden
   syrup

Topping
250 g (8 oz) cream cheese
^{1}/$_3$ cup (40 g/1^1/$_3$ oz) icing sugar
100 g (3^1/$_3$ oz) white chocolate,
   melted

➤ PREHEAT OVEN to moderate 180°C (350°F/Gas 4). Brush a 20 x 30 cm (8 x 12 inch) shallow tin with melted butter or oil. Line base and sides with baking paper.

1 Place oil, eggs and sugar in a large bowl. Whisk until well combined. Add flour, soda, cinnamon and cocoa; fold in chocolate and stir until combined.

2 Stir in carrot and syrup until smooth. Pour into tin; smooth surface. Bake 40 minutes or until skewer comes out clean if inserted in centre. Cool; spread with Topping. Decorate with ribbons of fresh carrot, if desired.

3 To make Topping: Using electric beaters, beat cream cheese and sugar until creamy. Add chocolate; beat until light and fluffy.

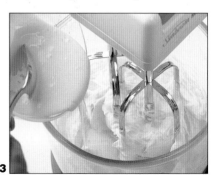

CHOCOLATE PEANUT SLICE

Preparation time: 35 minutes
Total cooking time: 20 minutes
Makes a 28 x 18 cm (11 x 7 inch) slice

250 g (8 oz) chocolate chip biscuits, finely crushed
70 g (2^1/$_3$ oz) butter, melted
50 g (1^2/$_3$ oz) butter, extra
^{1}/$_4$ cup (45 g/1^1/$_2$ oz) soft brown sugar
^{1}/$_4$ cup (80 g/2^2/$_3$ oz) condensed milk

2 eggs
1 cup (250 g/8 oz) smooth peanut butter
150 g (4^3/$_4$ oz) dark chocolate, melted
2 tablespoons cocoa powder

➤ PREHEAT OVEN to moderate 180°C (350°F/Gas 4). Line a 28 x 18 cm (11 x 7 inch) rectangular or lamington tin with enough baking paper to extend over the longest sides.

1 Combine biscuit crumbs and butter in medium bowl; mix well. Press mixture firmly into base of tin. Refrigerate 10–15 minutes or until firm.

2 Using electric beaters, beat butter and sugar until light and creamy. Add condensed milk, eggs and peanut butter; mix until smooth. Spread mixture evenly over biscuit base. Bake 15–20 minutes or until lightly golden. Leave in tin to cool.

3 Spread melted chocolate over cooled slice. Allow chocolate to set, then remove slice from tin. Using a sharp, flat-bladed knife, cut into bars. Dust with sifted cocoa powder or, if preferred, drizzle with 60 g (2 oz) of melted white chocolate. Store for up to two days in an airtight container in a cool, dry place.

1

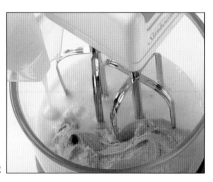

2

3

SOUR CREAM AND NUT SLICE

Preparation time: 20 minutes
Total cooking time: 35 minutes
Makes a 20 x 30 cm (8 x 12 inch) slice

1 cup (185 g/6 oz) brown sugar
$^3/_4$ cup (90 g/3 oz) plain flour
60 g (2 oz) ground almonds,
    pecans, walnuts or brazil nuts
$^1/_4$ cup (30 g/1 oz) cocoa powder
3 eggs
$^2/_3$ cup (160 g/5$^1/_4$ oz) sour
    cream
100 g (3$^1/_3$ oz) dark chocolate
150 g (4$^3/_4$ oz) butter, melted

Icing
200 g (6$^1/_2$ oz) milk chocolate
$^1/_3$ cup (90 g/3 oz) sour cream
$^2/_3$ cup (85 g/2$^3/_4$ oz) chopped
    walnuts

➤ PREHEAT OVEN to moderate 180°C (350°F/Gas 4). Brush a shallow 20 x 30 cm (8 x 12 inch) rectangular tin with melted butter or oil. Line base with baking paper, extending over two sides.

1 Place the sugar, flour, ground nuts, cocoa, eggs, sour cream, melted chocolate and butter in food processor bowl. Process 20 seconds or until well combined and mixture is smooth.

2 Pour mixture into prepared tin; smooth surface with knife. Bake 35 minutes or until skewer comes out clean when inserted in the centre. Leave slice in tin 10 minutes before turning onto wire rack to cool.

3 To make Icing: Chop chocolate and combine with cream in small pan. Stir over low heat until chocolate has melted and mixture is smooth. Cool slightly. Spread icing evenly over slice. Sprinkle chopped nuts over top. Cut into squares to serve.

COOK'S FILE

Storage: Make up to 4 days ahead.
Variation: Omit the ground nuts and increase the flour quantity to 1 cup (125 g/4 oz).

1

2

3

CHOCOLATE HAZELNUT SPIRALS

Preparation time: 20 minutes
Total cooking time: 10–12 minutes
Makes about 35

1$^1/_2$ cups (185 g/6 oz) plain
    flour
$^1/_2$ cup (60 g/2 oz) cocoa powder
$^1/_2$ cup (125 g/4 oz) caster sugar
$^1/_2$ cup (55 g/1$^3/_4$ oz) ground
    hazelnuts
100 g (3$^1/_3$ oz) butter, chopped
1 egg
1 tablespoon cold water,
    approximately

4 tablespoons chocolate hazelnut
    spread, at room temperature

➤ BRUSH TWO oven trays with melted butter or oil. Line with baking paper.

1 Place flour, cocoa, sugar and hazelnuts in food processor; add butter and process for 30 seconds or until mixture resembles fine crumbs. Add egg and enough water to moisten; process until mixture comes together. Turn dough onto lightly floured surface; knead 30 seconds or until smooth.

2 Roll dough out on a large sheet of baking paper, to form a rectangle 25 x 35 cm (10 x 14 inches). Trim uneven edges. Spread hazelnut spread evenly over dough. Using paper to lift dough, roll up from long side to form a log. Wrap tightly in paper and plastic wrap and refrigerate 30 minutes. Preheat oven to moderate 180°C (350°F/Gas 4).

3 Cut dough into 1 cm ($^1/_2$ inch) slices. Place onto prepared trays, allowing room for spreading. Bake for 10–12 minutes or until cooked through. Transfer to wire rack to cool.

COOK'S FILE

Variation: Ground almonds or walnuts can be used in place of hazelnuts.
Note: Chocolate hazelnut spread is available in most supermarkets and some delicatessens.

1

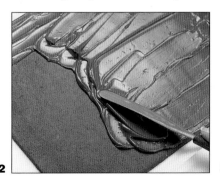

2

3

CHOCOLATE APRICOT COOKIES

Preparation time: 15 minutes
Total cooking time: 20 minutes
Makes about 40

125 g (4 oz) butter
$^{3}/_{4}$ cup (140 g/$4^{2}/_{3}$ oz) soft
   brown sugar
1 egg, lightly beaten
$^{1}/_{4}$ cup (30 g/1 oz) cocoa powder

$^{3}/_{4}$ cup (90 g/3 oz) self-raising
   flour
$^{1}/_{2}$ cup (60 g/2 oz) plain flour
$^{3}/_{4}$ cup (45 g/$1^{1}/_{2}$ oz) shredded
   coconut
1 cup (185 g/6 oz) chopped
   dried apricots (or other dried
   fruit)
$1^{1}/_{2}$ cups (265 g/$8^{1}/_{2}$ oz) dark
   choc bits

➤ PREHEAT OVEN to moderate
180°C (350°F/Gas 4). Line two oven
trays with baking paper.

1 Using electric beaters, beat butter
and sugar until light and creamy. Add
egg; beat until combined. Transfer to
a large bowl.

2 Stir in sifted cocoa and flours,
coconut, apricots and choc bits. Mix to
a firm dough.

3 Roll level tablespoons of mixture
into rounds. Place on prepared trays;
flatten slightly. Bake 15–20 minutes
or until golden. Transfer to a wire
rack to cool.

FRUITY CHOCOLATE SLICE

Preparation time: 15 minutes +
   30 minutes refrigeration
Total cooking time: 5 minutes
Makes a 20 x 30 cm (8 x 12 inch) slice

250 g (8 oz) chocolate cream
   biscuits, crushed
$^{1}/_{2}$ cup (45 g/$1^{1}/_{2}$ oz) desiccated
   coconut
$^{1}/_{2}$ cup (about 60 g/2 oz) roughly
   chopped pecans or walnuts
$^{1}/_{2}$ cup (95 g/$3^{1}/_{4}$ oz) chopped
   dried apricots
$^{1}/_{4}$ cup (55 g/$1^{3}/_{4}$ oz) chopped
   glacé pineapple
$^{1}/_{4}$ cup (60 g/2 oz) chopped
   glacé cherries

$^{1}/_{4}$ cup (30 g/1 oz) sultanas
2 tablespoons cocoa powder
150 g ($4^{3}/_{4}$ oz) dark cooking
   chocolate, roughly chopped
80 g ($2^{2}/_{3}$ oz) butter
2 tablespoons golden syrup
1 egg, lightly beaten

Icing
150 g ($4^{3}/_{4}$ oz) dark chocolate,
   chopped
60 g (2 oz) butter

➤ BRUSH A 20 x 30 cm (8 x 12 inch)
rectangular or lamington tin with
melted butter or oil. Line base and
sides of tin with baking paper extending over 2 sides.

1 Combine biscuit crumbs, coconut,
nuts, fruits and cocoa in medium
mixing bowl; make a well in centre.

2 Combine chocolate, butter and
syrup in a small heavy-based pan. Stir
over low heat until the chocolate and
butter have melted and mixture is
smooth. Remove from heat. Pour
chocolate mixture over fruit mixture;
add egg. Stir until well combined.
Press into tin and smooth surface.
Refrigerate 30 minutes or until firm.

3 To make Icing: Place chocolate
and butter in small heatproof bowl.
Stand bowl over pan of simmering
water. Stir until chocolate and butter
have melted and mixture is smooth.
Cool until thickened slightly.
Spread evenly over slice. Refrigerate
until set. Remove slice from the tin.
Using a sharp knife, cut into small
squares or bars. Store in an airtight
container in the refrigerator for up to
two weeks.

Chocolate Apricot Cookies (top) and
Fruity Chocolate Slice

CHOCOLATE CHEESECAKE SLICE

Preparation time: 40 minutes
+ 30 minutes refrigeration
Total cooking time: 30 minutes
Makes a 20 x 30 cm (8 x 12 inch) slice

1¹/₂ cups (200 g/6¹/₂ oz) plain
    chocolate biscuit crumbs
80 g (2²/₃ oz) butter, melted
100 g (3¹/₃ oz) chocolate dots

Filling
375 g (12 oz) cream cheese
¹/₂ cup (125 g/4 oz) sugar
3 eggs
150 g (4³/₄ oz) white chocolate,
    melted

Topping
150 g (4³/₄ oz) dark cooking
    chocolate, melted
²/₃ cup (160 g/5¹/₄ oz) sour
    cream

➤PREHEAT OVEN to moderate 180°C (350°F/Gas 4). Brush a 20 x 30 cm (8 x 12 inch) rectangular or lamington tin with melted butter or oil. Line with baking paper extending over longer sides.

1 Combine biscuit crumbs and butter in bowl; stir until combined. Press mixture into base of prepared tin. Sprinkle evenly with chocolate dots.

2 To make Filling: Using electric beaters, beat cream cheese in small bowl until creamy; beat in sugar until smooth. Add eggs, gradually, beating well after each addition. Add the chocolate; beat until smooth. Spread mixture over prepared base. Bake for 30 minutes or until just set. Cool, cover and refrigerate until firm.

3 To make Topping: Combine chocolate and sour cream in a small bowl; stand over a pan of simmering water. Stir until chocolate has melted and mixture is smooth. Spread evenly over the cheesecake, marking regular lines with a flat-bladed knife. Refrigerate until firm. Cut into slices.

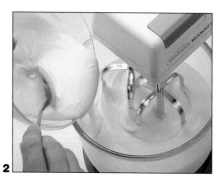

CHOC-COATED CARAMEL FILLED BISCUITS

Preparation time: 40 minutes
Total cooking time: 5 minutes
Makes about 30

250 g (8 oz) Jersey caramels
20 g (²/₃ oz) butter
1 tablespoon cream
375 g (12 oz) Morning Coffee
  biscuits (1¹/₂ packets)
450 g (14¹/₃ oz) dark chocolate
  melts

40 g (1¹/₃ oz) white vegetable
  shortening (copha)

➤ LINE TWO oven trays with foil.
1 Combine caramels, butter and cream in small pan. Stir over low heat until caramels have melted and the mixture is smooth. Cool slightly until mixture begins to thicken.
2 Sandwich two biscuits together with 1 teaspoon of caramel mixture. Repeat using remaining caramel and biscuits. Stand about 15 minutes or until caramel firms.
3 Combine chocolate and shortening in small bowl; stand bowl over pan of simmering water. Stir until chocolate and shortening have melted and the mixture is smooth. Using two forks, dip biscuits into chocolate; drain excess chocolate and place on prepared trays to set.

COOK'S FILE

Storage time: Store in airtight container in cool place or in refrigerator for up to three days.
Hint: Use any kind of plain sweet biscuits for this recipe. Use round biscuits, if preferred.

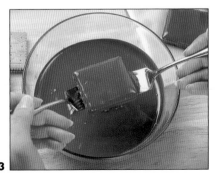

TWO-TONE CHOC-CHIP BISCUITS

Preparation time: 15 minutes
Total cooking time: 12–15 minutes
Makes about 40

125 g (4 oz) butter
1¹/₂ cups (280 g/9 oz) brown
  sugar
2 teaspoons vanilla essence
2 eggs, lightly beaten
1 teaspoon bicarbonate of soda

2¹/₂ cups (310 g/9³/₄ oz) plain
  flour
150 g (4³/₄ oz) dark choc bits
150 g (4³/₄ oz) white choc bits

➤ PREHEAT OVEN to moderate 180°C (350°F/Gas 4). Brush two oven trays with melted butter or oil. Line with baking paper.

1 Using electric beaters, beat butter, sugar and essence in small bowl until light and creamy. Add eggs gradually, beating well after each addition. Transfer to a large bowl.

2 Using a metal spoon, fold soda, sifted flour and choc bits into creamed mixture; mix until smooth.

3 Drop level tablespoons of mixture onto prepared trays, allowing for spreading; flatten mixture slightly. Bake 12–15 minutes or until lightly browned and cooked through. Transfer to wire rack to cool.

COOK'S FILE

Hint: Chopped dark and white block chocolate can be used instead of choc bits.

MACADAMIA NUT AND WHITE CHOC BROWNIES

Preparation time: 20 minutes
Total cooking time: 40 minutes
Makes 20 squares

200 g (6¹/₂ oz) dark cooking
 chocolate, chopped
100 g (3¹/₃ oz) butter
2 tablespoons water
¹/₂ cup (125 g/4 oz) caster sugar
2 teaspoons vanilla essence

2 eggs, lightly beaten
¹/₃ cup (40 g/1¹/₃ oz) plain flour
150 g (4³/₄ oz) white chocolate
²/₃ cup (90 g/3 oz) chopped
 macadamia nuts

►PREHEAT OVEN to moderate 180°C (350°F/Gas 4). Line a 20 cm (8 inch) square cake tin with foil or baking paper.

1 Combine chocolate, butter and water in a medium pan. Stir over low heat until chocolate and butter have melted and mixture is smooth. Stir in sugar; remove from heat. Stir in the vanilla essence, eggs and flour; mix until well combined.

2 Using a sharp knife, chop white chocolate into large chunks. Stir chocolate and nuts into mixture. (Stop stirring as soon as chocolate begins to melt.) Spoon mixture into tin. Bake for 35 minutes or until top is firm to touch. Cool in tin. Cut into squares.

COOK'S FILE

Storage time: Store in an airtight container for up to three days.

DESSERTS

CHOCOLATE BASKETS WITH HONEYCOMB ICE-CREAM

Preparation time: 40 minutes + freezing
Total cooking time: 2–3 minutes
Serves 8

4 x 50 g (1²/₃ oz) chocolate-coated honeycomb bars
200 g (6¹/₂ oz) dark chocolate melts
2 litre carton good-quality vanilla ice-cream

➤ PLACE EIGHT small upturned drinking glasses or upturned glass jars on work area. Cut some plastic freezer wrap into 8 x 14 cm (3 x 5¹/₂ inch) square sheets (see Note).

1 Using a sharp knife, roughly chop honeycomb bars; set aside.

2 Soften the ice-cream slightly; transfer to a large bowl; stir in honeycomb chocolate pieces. Return mixture to ice-cream container; freeze until firm.

3 Place chocolate in small heatproof bowl; stand bowl over pan of simmering water. Stir until chocolate has melted and mixture is smooth. Remove from heat. Working with one sheet at a time, spread a circle of melted chocolate on freezer wrap. Drape each square over a glass or jar, chocolate side out.

4 Allow chocolate to set, then carefully peel away plastic. Scoop ice-cream into the chocolate cups. Decorate with long chocolate curls, if desired.

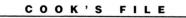
COOK'S FILE

Storage time: Ice-cream can be kept for one month in freezer.

Note: Plastic freezer wrap is heavier than standard plastic wrap. It is available in most supermarkets, where it is often sold under the name of freezer go-between.

Hint: If the weather is warm, Chocolate Baskets may need to be refrigerated in order to set.

DARK CHOCOLATE PUDDING WITH MOCHA SAUCE

Preparation time: 30 minutes
Total cooking time: 1 hour 25 minutes
Serves 6

1¼ cups (155 g/5 oz) self-raising flour
1 cup (125 g/4 oz) plain flour
¼ cup (30 g/1 oz) cocoa powder
¼ teaspoon bicarbonate of soda
150 g (4¾ oz) butter
½ cup (125 g/4 oz) caster sugar
¼ cup (45 g/1½ oz) soft dark brown sugar
100 g (3⅓ oz) dark chocolate, chopped
1 teaspoon vanilla essence
2 eggs, lightly beaten
¾ cup (185 ml/6 fl oz) buttermilk
1 cup (175 g/5⅔ oz) dark choc bits

Mocha Sauce
50 g (1⅔ oz) butter
150 g (4¾ oz) dark chocolate, chopped
1½ cups (375 ml/12 fl oz) cream
1 tablespoon instant coffee powder
1–2 tablespoons crème de cacao

➤ BRUSH AN 8-cup capacity pudding basin or steamer with melted butter or oil. Line base with paper; grease paper. Grease a large sheet of aluminium foil and a large sheet of greaseproof paper. Lay the paper over the foil, greased side up. Pleat paper in the centre. Set aside.

1 Sift flours, cocoa and soda into a large mixing bowl. Make a well in the centre. Combine butter, sugars, chocolate and essence in a pan. Stir over low heat until butter and chocolate have melted and sugars have dissolved; remove from heat. Add the butter mixture, beaten eggs and buttermilk to flour mixture. Using a wooden spoon, stir until well combined. Stir in choc bits.

2 Spoon mixture into prepared basin. Cover with the greased foil and paper, greased side down. Place lid over foil and secure clips. (If you have no lid, lay a pleated tea-towel over foil; tie securely with string under the lip of the basin. Knot the four corners of the tea-towel together; use as a handle to help lower the basin into the pan.)

Place the basin on a trivet in a large, deep pan. Carefully pour boiling water down the side of the pan to come halfway up the side of the basin. Bring to the boil; cover and cook for 1 hour 15 minutes. Do not let pudding boil dry; replenish with boiling water as pudding is cooking. When cooked, remove covering and invert onto a plate. Serve hot with Mocha Sauce.

3 To make Mocha Sauce: Combine butter, chocolate, cream and coffee powder in a small pan. Stir over low heat until the butter and chocolate have melted and the mixture is smooth. Add crème de cacao, stir until well combined; remove from heat. Serve immediately.

1

2

3

CHOCOLATE MOUSSE

Preparation time: 20 minutes
Total cooking time: Nil
Makes 4

250 g (8 oz) dark chocolate
3 eggs
1/4 cup (60 g/2 oz) caster sugar
2 teaspoons dark rum
1 cup (250 ml/8 fl oz) cream,
    whipped to soft peaks

➤ PLACE CHOCOLATE in a small heatproof bowl; stir over a pan of simmering water until chocolate has melted and mixture is smooth. Set aside to cool.

1 Using electric beaters, beat eggs and sugar in a small bowl for 5 minutes or until thick, pale and increased in volume.

2 Transfer mixture to a large bowl. Using a metal spoon, fold melted chocolate and rum into the egg mixture, then fold in whipped cream. Work quickly and lightly until mixture is just combined.

3 Spoon mousse into four 1-cup capacity ramekins or four dessert glasses. Refrigerate 2 hours or until mousse has set. Decorate with chocolate leaves, if desired. (See Note.)

COOK'S FILE

Storage time: Chocolate Mousse will keep for two days in the refrigerator. Cover surface with plastic wrap to prevent a skin forming.

Note: *To make chocolate leaves:* Melt required amount of dark chocolate. With a clean paintbrush, paint melted chocolate evenly over firm, well-defined leaves, such as rose, oak or ivy. Lay aside to set. Gently peel away leaf (not chocolate) when firm. Keep refrigerated until needed.

1

2

3

GATEAU FORESTIERE

Preparation time: 1 hour 30 minutes
Total cooking time: 1 hour 30 minutes
Makes one 20 cm (8 inch) round cake

125 g (4 oz) butter
3/4 cup (140 g/4²/3 oz) soft
   brown sugar
1/3 cup (90 g/3 oz) caster sugar
2 eggs, lightly beaten
1 teaspoon vanilla essence
1/2 cup (60 g/2 oz) plain flour
3/4 cup (90 g/3 oz) self-raising
   flour
1 teaspoon bicarbonate of soda
1/3 cup (40 g/1¹/3 oz) cocoa
   powder
1/4 cup (60 ml/2 fl oz) hot water
1 cup (250 ml/8 fl oz)
   buttermilk
chocolate caraque curls, for
   decoration

Buttercream
300 g (9²/3 oz) unsalted butter
2/3 cup (85 g/2³/4 oz) icing
   sugar, sifted
2–3 drops peppermint essence
2–3 drops green food colouring
125 g (4 oz) dark chocolate,
   melted

Meringue Mushrooms
2 egg whites
3/4 cup (90 g/3 oz) icing sugar,
   sifted
1 teaspoon lemon juice

➤ PREHEAT OVEN to moderate 180°C (350°F/Gas Mark 4). Brush a deep 20 cm (8 inch) round cake tin with melted butter or oil. Line base with baking paper.

1 Beat butter and sugars in a large bowl until light and creamy. Add eggs gradually, beating well after each addition. Add essence; beat until combined. Transfer mixture to large bowl.

2 Using a metal spoon, fold in sifted flours, soda and cocoa alternately with water and milk. Stir 1 minute until well combined.

3 Spoon mixture into prepared tin; smooth surface. Bake 45–50 minutes or until skewer comes out clean when inserted in centre. Leave cake in tin for 20 minutes before turning onto a wire rack to cool.

4 To make Buttercream: Using electric beaters, beat butter and sugar in small bowl until light and creamy. Transfer one-third of the mixture to small bowl. Add peppermint essence and mix well. Reserve 1 tablespoon and tint with green food colouring. Add the chocolate to the remaining Buttercream; beat until well combined.

5 To make Meringue Mushrooms: Preheat the oven to slow 150°C (300°F/Gas 2). Brush two oven trays with melted butter or oil. Line with baking paper. Place egg whites in small bowl; beat until firm peaks form. Add sugar gradually, beating until mixture is thick and glossy. Add juice; continue beating until sugar has dissolved. Place meringue mixture in a piping bag fitted with plain round nozzle. Pipe three-quarters of mixture into 2 cm (³/4 inch) rounds; pipe the remaining quarter into small 5 mm (¹/4 inch) rounds. Smooth peaks with a wet finger. Bake 20–30 minutes (until pale and crisp). Turn oven off. Cool in oven, with oven door ajar. When cool, use a small amount of the Buttercream to attach mushroom caps to stalks.

To assemble Gateau: Cut dome from cake to make a level surface. Turn cake upside-down and cut into three horizontal layers. Place base layer on serving plate and spread with half of the mint cream. Top with next layer and spread top with remaining mint cream. Place third layer on top. Using a flat-bladed knife, spread Chocolate Buttercream evenly over top and sides of cake. Arrange Meringue Mushrooms on top of cake; dust with sifted cocoa powder. Place chocolate caraque curls vertically around outside of cake. (See page 6 for instructions on how to make curls.) Spoon the green mint cream into paper icing bag; seal end and snip off tip in a V-shape. Pipe green leaves around mushrooms.

1

2

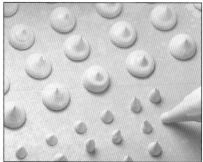

CHOCOLATE ORANGE TARTS

Preparation time: 45 minutes
+ 20 minutes refrigeration
Total cooking time: 45–50 minutes
Serves 6

³/4 cup (90 g/3 oz) plain flour,
  sifted
¹/4 cup (45 g/1¹/2 oz) rice flour,
  sifted
pinch salt
¹/2 cup (95 g/3¹/4 oz) ground
  almonds
1 tablespoon sugar
125 g (4 oz) butter, chopped
1 egg yolk
1–2 tablespoons cold water
whipped cream, for serving
candied orange rind, for serving

Filling
100 g (3¹/3 oz) dark chocolate,
  chopped
125 g (4 oz) milk chocolate,
  chopped
1 teaspoon grated orange rind
2 tablespoons orange juice
1¹/4 cups (315 ml/10 fl oz)
  cream
2 eggs
3 egg yolks, whisked

► PREHEAT OVEN to moderate 180°C (350°F/Gas 4). Brush six 12-cm (5 inch) individual fluted flan tins with melted butter.

1 Place flours, salt, almonds, sugar and butter in food processor. Process 20 seconds or until mixture is fine and crumbly. Add egg yolk and enough water to combine all ingredients. Process mixture until it comes together. Divide mixture into 6 even portions. Roll out between two sheets of baking paper to 6 mm (¹/4 inch) thickness.

Place into tart tins and refrigerate for 20 minutes; trim edges with a knife.

2 Cut 6 sheets of greaseproof paper large enough to cover pastry-lined tins. Lay paper over pastry; spread with an even layer of dried beans or rice. Bake 15 minutes; discard rice and paper and bake another 5 minutes.

3 To make Filling: Place chocolate in heatproof bowl; stand bowl over a

pan of simmering water; stir until chocolate melts. Remove from heat. Whisk orange rind, juice, cream, eggs and egg yolks in a jug until combined. Gradually add to melted chocolate, whisking constantly. Pour into cases and bake 20–25 minutes or until just set. (Filling will set more as tarts cool.) Serve warm or cold with whipped cream and candied orange rind.

CHOCOLATE FUDGE PUDDINGS

Preparation time: 40 minutes
+ 20 minutes standing
Total cooking time: 40 minutes
Serves 6

150 g (4³/₄ oz) dark chocolate,
    roughly chopped
¹/₂ cup (125 ml/4 fl oz) milk
1 cup (80 g/2²/₃ oz) stale white
    breadcrumbs, firmly packed
30 g (1 oz) unsalted butter
1 tablespoon sugar
2 eggs, separated
¹/₄ cup (25 g/³/₄ oz) walnuts,
    finely chopped
¹/₂ teaspoon vanilla essence

Hot Chocolate Sauce
185 g (6 oz) dark chocolate,
    roughly chopped
²/₃ cup (170 ml/5¹/₂ fl oz) cream

➤ PREHEAT OVEN to moderate
180°C (350°F/Gas 4). Brush six ¹/₄-cup capacity dariole moulds or ramekins with melted butter. Line bases with baking paper.

1 Place chocolate and milk in medium pan and stir over medium heat until combined. Remove from heat and stir in breadcrumbs. Stand 20 minutes, then transfer to a bowl.

2 Using electric beaters, beat butter and sugar until light and creamy. Add yolks gradually, beating well after each addition. Fold into chocolate mixture. Stir in walnuts and vanilla.

3 Using electric beaters, beat the egg whites until stiff peaks form. Fold into the chocolate mixture. Spoon the mixture into prepared dishes. Place in a baking dish and pour in enough boiling water to come halfway up the sides of dishes. Lightly grease some foil and rest on top of the dishes. Bake for 35 minutes or until just set. Leave to stand for 5 minutes before turning out onto serving plates. Pour the Hot Chocolate Sauce over puddings. Serve with thick cream,. if desired.

4 To make the Hot Chocolate Sauce: Place chocolate and cream in a small heatproof bowl; stand bowl over a pan of simmering water; stir until chocolate melts and mixture is smooth. Serve immediately.

COOK'S FILE

Hint: Serve the puddings dusted with a combination of icing sugar and cocoa, if desired. Sauce can be served separately in a jug.

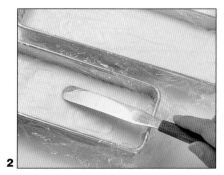

FROZEN CHOCOLATE AND BERRY CHEQUERBOARD PARFAIT

Preparation time: 40 minutes +
  3 hours freezing
Total cooking time: Nil
Serves 10–12

White Layer
200 g (6¹/₂ oz) white chocolate, melted
³/₄ cup (185 ml/6 fl oz) cream
2 eggs, separated

Berry Layer
300 g (9²/₃ oz) fresh or frozen strawberries or raspberries
150 g (4³/₄ oz) white chocolate, melted
1 tablespoon caster sugar
¹/₄ cup (60 ml/2 fl oz) cream

2 eggs, separated
¹/₂ cup (125 ml/4 fl oz) thickened cream, extra
1 egg white, extra, beaten

Berry Sauce
500 g (1 lb) fresh or frozen strawberries or raspberries
2 teaspoons caster sugar
¹/₂ cup (125 ml/4 fl oz) water, approximately

➤ COVER BASE and sides of two 8 x 26 cm (3 x 10¹/₂ inch) bar tins with plastic wrap or foil. (Thaw frozen berries completely before beginning.)
1 To make White Layer: Combine chocolate, ¹/₄ cup cream and egg yolks in medium bowl; mix well. In a separate bowl, whip remaining cream until soft peaks form. Fold into chocolate mixture. Beat egg whites in clean, dry bowl until soft peaks form.
2 Using a metal spoon gently fold

white into chocolate mixture. Divide mixture evenly between prepared bar tins. Smooth surface with flat-bladed knife. Cover; freeze until firm.
3 To make Berry Layer: Process berries until smooth. Combine in medium bowl with chocolate, sugar, cream and egg yolks; stir until smooth. Beat extra cream until soft peaks form; gently fold into chocolate mixture. Beat egg whites in clean, dry bowl with electric mixer until soft

peaks form. Gently fold white into chocolate mixture. Divide mixture between tins; spread evenly over frozen white layer. Cover with plastic wrap and freeze until firm.

4 *To assemble Parfait:* Turn one mousse bar onto a work surface. (You may need to gently loosen bar with a flat-bladed knife.) Working quickly, cut lengthways into 4 even slices. Turn 2 slices upside-down. Brush the surfaces with egg white. Place upside-down slices on remaining slices for chequerboard pattern. Freeze while preparing second bar in same way.

5 Turn both bars onto work surface, one of them upside-down. Brush tops with egg white; join bars together. Cover Parfait tightly with plastic wrap, press bars together gently but firmly. Return to freezer for another hour. Serve Chequerboard Parfait sliced with Berry Sauce.

6 **To make Berry Sauce**: Blend or process berries, sugar and water until smooth, adding enough water to make a thick pouring consistency.

COOK'S FILE

Storage time: Dessert can be frozen for up to two months, sealed in plastic wrap. Sauce can be made a day ahead. Store, covered, in refrigerator.

Hint: If using any other berry with large seeds, sieve purées before adding to chocolate mixtures or sauce.

WHITE CHOCOLATE PUFFS WITH DARK CHOCOLATE SAUCE

Preparation time: 40 minutes
Total cooking time: 35 minutes
Serves 4–6

$^3/_4$ cup (185 ml/6 fl oz) water
60 g (2 oz) butter
$^3/_4$ cup (90 g/3 oz) plain flour
3 eggs, beaten
$^1/_4$ cup (30 g/1 oz) custard
  powder
1 tablespoon caster sugar
$1^1/_2$ cups (375 ml/12 fl oz) milk
150 g ($4^3/_4$ oz) white chocolate
  melts, chopped

1 tablespoon Grand Marnier

Chocolate Sauce
125 g (4 oz) dark chocolate,
  chopped
$^1/_2$ cup (125 ml/4 fl oz) cream

▶ PREHEAT OVEN to hot 210°C (415°F/Gas 6-7). Line an oven tray with baking paper.
1 Heat water and butter in pan; bring to boil, remove from heat. Add flour. Stir over heat until mixture forms a smooth ball. Allow to cool slightly. Place mixture in food processor. With motor constantly operating, gradually add eggs to form a smooth thick paste. Spoon 2 heaped teaspoons of mixture on tray 5 cm (2 inches) apart.

Sprinkle with water. Bake 10 minutes. Reduce heat to moderate 180°C (350°F/Gas 4); bake 12–15 minutes or until dough is puffed. Cut slit in each. Turn off oven, cool 5 minutes.
2 Combine custard powder and sugar in pan; gradually add milk, stirring until smooth. Stir over low heat until mixture boils and thickens. Remove from heat; add chocolate and liqueur. Stir until melted. Cover surface with plastic wrap; cool.
3 Stir custard until smooth, spoon into a piping bag fitted with a 1 cm ($^1/_2$ inch) plain nozzle. Pipe into each puff. Serve with warm Chocolate Sauce.
4 To make Chocolate Sauce: Combine chocolate and cream in pan; stir over low heat until melted.

DECADENT WHITE CHOCOLATE MARQUIS MOUSSE

Preparation time: 40 minutes
  + 3 hours refrigeration
Total cooking time: 5 minutes
Serves 6

60 g (2 oz) dark cooking
  chocolate, melted
4 egg yolks
1/2 cup (125 g/4 oz) caster sugar
1 tablespoon honey
1 teaspoon instant coffee
  powder
2 teaspoons water
200 g (6 1/2 oz) white chocolate,
  melted
125 g (4 oz) butter
2/3 cup (170 ml/5 1/2 fl oz) thick
  cream

Praline
1/2 cup (80 g/2 2/3 oz) blanched
  almonds, toasted

1/2 cup (125 g/4 oz) caster sugar
1/3 cup (80 ml/2 3/4 fl oz) water

➤ PLACE CHOCOLATE in small
paper piping bag.
1 Pipe chocolate in a swirling pattern
over the inside surface of 6 dessert
glasses; place in refrigerator and
allow to set.
2 Using electric beaters, beat yolks,
sugar, honey and blended coffee and
water in small bowl until very thick.
Beat in white chocolate until smooth.
In another bowl, beat butter with electric beaters until light and creamy.
Add egg yolk mixture; beat until
smooth. Transfer to a medium bowl.
3 Beat cream until soft peaks form.
Using a metal spoon, gently fold
cream into chocolate mixture. Fold in
finely chopped or processed praline.
Spoon mixture into dessert glasses.
Refrigerate 2–3 hours. Serve with
large praline pieces. Top with
whipped cream, if desired.
4 To make Praline: Line an oven
tray with baking paper. Spread with

almonds. Combine sugar and water in
small pan; stir over low heat, without
boiling, until sugar has dissolved.
Brush edges of pan with water; bring
to boil; reduce heat. Simmer, without
stirring, until golden. Remove from
heat immediately and pour carefully
over almonds. Allow to set until hard.
Break half into pieces for topping.
Chop or process remainder into
fine crumbs. Mousse is best eaten on
the day it is made.

RICH FROZEN DESSERT CAKE

Preparation time: 20 minutes +
  overnight freezing
Total cooking time: 25 minutes
Makes one 23 cm (9 inch) round cake

500 g (1 lb) dark cooking
  chocolate
150 g (4³/4 oz) butter
¹/2 cup (95 g/3¹/4 oz) ground
  almonds
5 eggs

2 tablespoons caster sugar
2 tablespoons plain flour
1 cup (250 g/8 oz) sour cream
150 g (4³/4 oz) milk chocolate,
  melted

➤PREHEAT OVEN to moderate
180°C (350°F/Gas 4). Brush a 23 cm
(9 inch) springform tin with melted
butter or oil. Line base and sides with
baking paper.
1 Combine chocolate and butter in
small pan; stir over low heat until
chocolate and butter have melted. Stir
in almonds and transfer to a large

bowl. Using electric beaters, beat eggs
and sugar until thick. Fold in flour.
2 Fold egg mixture into chocolate
mixture; spoon into prepared tin. Bake
25 minutes or until top of cake is just
set. Remove from oven, cool. Cover
with plastic wrap, and freeze in tin
overnight or until firm.
3 Place sour cream in small bowl;
whisk chocolate into sour cream until
smooth. Spread over top of cake.
Freeze, covered, until firm. Top with
large chocolate scrolls and serve, cut
into wedges, with whipped cream or
ice-cream, if desired.

CHOCOLATE PEAR PANCAKE

Preparation time: 20 minutes
Total cooking time: 10–12 minutes
Serves 2–4

1 large pear
40 g (1¹/3 oz) butter
1 teaspoon ground cinnamon
1 tablespoon soft brown sugar
1 tablespoon caster sugar
3 eggs, separated
2 teaspoons caster sugar, extra
¹/4 cup (30 g/1 oz) self-raising
  flour
1 tablespoon cocoa powder

¹/4 cup (60 ml/2 fl oz) milk

➤PEEL AND quarter pear. Remove
core; slice thinly.
1 Combine butter, cinnamon and
sugars in 16 cm (6¹/2 inch) round non-
stick frying pan. Stir over medium
heat until butter has melted and sugar
has dissolved. Add pear slices, arrang-
ing them in an overlapping pattern
around the base of the pan. Simmer
1–2 minutes or until pear is just
tender. Remove from heat.
2 Using electric beaters, beat egg
whites until soft peaks form.
Gradually add extra sugar; beat until
combined. In a separate bowl, beat egg
yolks, sifted flour and cocoa and milk
until smooth. Using a metal spoon,

fold in egg whites; stir to combine.
3 Return pan to heat. Gently pour the
pancake mixture over the pears. Cook
over medium-low heat 3–4 minutes or
until mixture begins to rise like a
soufflé. (The pancake should be fluffy
and sponge-like in texture, and should
spring back when lightly touched.)
Remove pan from heat and place
under the preheated hot grill. Cook for
1–2 minutes or until the top has just
turned golden brown. Turn the pancake onto serving plate, cut into
wedges and serve immediately with
ice-cream, if desired. (Pancakes will
deflate very quickly so serve as soon
as they are cooked.) Serve with
whipped cream, chocolate sauce and
roasted hazelnuts, if preferred.

*Rich Frozen Dessert Cake (top) and
Chocolate Pear Pancake*

CHOCOLATE SOUFFLE

Preparation time: 15 minutes
Total cooking time: 15 minutes
Serves 6

30 g (1 oz) butter
2 tablespoons plain flour
1 cup (250 ml/8 fl oz) milk
150 g (4³⁄₄ oz) dark Toblerone
    chocolate, chopped
4 eggs, separated
1 egg white, extra

➤ PREHEAT OVEN to hot 210°C (415°F/Gas 6–7). Grease 6 individual ramekin dishes with melted butter, dust with caster sugar to form a crusty coating; shake off excess. Wrap length of foil or baking paper around the ramekins to form a collar and secure with string.

1 Heat butter in small pan; add flour. Stir over low heat 2 minutes or until flour is lightly golden and bubbling. Gradually add milk, stirring until mixture is smooth. Stir constantly over medium heat until mixture boils and thickens. Remove from heat; add chocolate and stir until melted. Cool slightly. Stir in lightly beaten egg yolks; whisk until smooth.

2 Using electric beaters, beat egg whites in a large dry, clean bowl until soft peaks form. Using a metal spoon, fold into chocolate mixture in two batches. Divide the mixture evenly between the ramekins. Run a knife in a circle 1 cm (¹⁄₂ inch) from edge of dish, through the mixture, taking care not to touch bottom of dish. Place dishes on oven tray. Bake 15 minutes. Serve immediately. Dust with icing sugar, if desired.

COOK'S FILE

Storage time: Can be prepared ahead up to step 2. Cover the surface of the sauce with plastic wrap to prevent a skin forming.

1

2

3

CHOCOLATE AND CARAMEL NUT TARTS

Preparation time: 40 minutes
Total cooking time: 20 minutes
Serves 6

2 cups (250 g/8 oz) plain flour
200 g (6¹/₂ oz) chilled butter,
    chopped
1 egg
2–3 tablespoons iced water

Filling
110 g (3²/₃ oz) butter
³/₄ cup (140 g/4²/₃ oz) soft
    brown sugar
¹/₄ cup (90 g/3 oz) golden syrup
1 teaspoon vanilla essence
70 g (2¹/₃ oz) dark chocolate
1 egg, lightly beaten
¹/₃ cup (50 g/1²/₃ oz) pine nuts
1 cup (100 g/3¹/₃ oz) pecan nuts

➤ BRUSH SIX 11-cm (4¹/₂ inch) diameter shallow individual fluted flan tins with melted butter or oil.

1 Place flour and butter in food processor. Process until fine and crumbly. Add egg and almost all the water; process again until mixture comes together, adding more water if necessary. Turn onto lightly floured surface; press together until smooth. Wrap in plastic and refrigerate 15–20 minutes.

2 Preheat oven to moderate 180°C (350°F/Gas 4). Divide pastry into 6 equal portions. Roll each portion between greaseproof paper to fit prepared tins Line base and sides of tin with pastry; trim edges. Re-roll remaining pastry scraps into a rectangle. Using a small sharp knife or fluted pastry wheel, cut into long, thin strips and set aside.

3 To make Filling: Combine butter, sugar, syrup, vanilla and chocolate in medium pan. Stir over medium heat until butter and chocolate have melted and sugar has dissolved. Remove from heat; cool slightly. Whisk in egg. Stir through pine nuts and pecans. Spoon mixture evenly into pastry cases.

4 Brush reserved pastry strips with milk or lightly beaten egg. Lay strips over each tart in a crisscross-cross pattern. Press edges to seal. Trim with a sharp knife. Bake 10–15 minutes. Leave tarts in tins 5 minutes before removing. Dust with icing sugar, if desired. Can be served warm with thick cream or ice-cream. If preferred, may be served cold.

CHOCOLATE MOUSSE FLAN

Preparation time: 35 minutes
+ 20 minutes refrigeration
Total cooking time:Nil
Makes one 23 cm (9 inch) round flan

200 g (6¹/₂ oz) chocolate biscuit
    crumbs
100 g (3¹/₃ oz) butter, melted

Chocolate Cream
100 g (3¹/₃ oz) dark cooking
    chocolate
¹/₄ cup (60 ml/2 fl oz) cream
cocoa powder, for dusting

Mocha Mousse
200 g (6¹/₂ oz) dark cooking
    chocolate, melted
60 g (2 oz) butter, melted
¹/₄ cup (60 ml/2 fl oz) thick
    cream
2 egg yolks
2 teaspoons instant coffee
    powder
1 teaspoon boiling water
2 teaspoons gelatine
1 tablespoon water
³/₄ cup (185 ml/6 fl oz) thick
    cream, extra

➤BRUSH A 23 cm (9 inch) fluted, round, loose-bottomed flan tin with melted butter or oil.

1 Combine the biscuit crumbs and butter in a small bowl; mix well. Press mixture into base and sides of tin. Refrigerate 20 minutes or until firm.

2 To make Chocolate Cream: Place chocolate and cream in small heatproof bowl; stand bowl over pan of simmering water until chocolate melts and mixture is smooth. Spread evenly over base of prepared flan. Refrigerate until set.

3 To make Mocha Mousse: Combine chocolate, butter, cream and yolks in medium bowl; mix well. Add combined coffee and boiling water.

4 Sprinkle gelatine over water in small bowl. Stand bowl in a pan of hot water, stirring until gelatine dissolves. Add gelatine mixture to chocolate mixture; stir with a wooden spoon until smooth.

5 Using electric beaters, beat cream in large bowl until soft peaks form. Using a metal spoon, fold into chocolate mixture. Spread over prepared flan. Refrigerate until set.

6 Cut a stencil from stiff cardboard (see Note). Place stencil over flan, dust with cocoa powder; carefully lift off stencil. Serve flan in wedges with cream or ice-cream, if desired.

COOK'S FILE

Storage time: Mousse Flan can be made a day ahead. Store in airtight container. Dust with cocoa powder just before serving.

Notes: To make cardboard stencil, draw a geometric pattern on a sheet of stiff cardboard; cut out pattern with a sharp scalpel. (Remove all residual cardboard particles before putting on cake.) Alternatively, buy a plastic stencil from a craft shop. Some of these stencils come in fancy designs, such as lace, stars or animal shapes—any of which will give a distinctive finish to a simple cake or dessert.

Cocoa powder is available in a variety of forms and degrees of quality. Dark cocoa powder from Holland is considered to be the best–it has a deep colour, a mild taste and dissolves easily. It can be used when cocoa powder is to be used in large quantities such as this flan, or when making truffles. Dark cocoa powder is available from delicatessens or the gourmet section of supermarkets.

4

5

6

MOCHA ICE-CREAM

Preparation time: 20 minute + freezing
Total cooking time: 10–15 minutes
Makes about 2 litres

1/2 cup (40 g/1 1/3 oz) espresso
    coffee beans
3 cups (750 ml/24 fl oz) cream
250 g (8 oz) dark cooking
    chocolate, chopped
3/4 cup (185 g/6 oz) caster sugar
6 egg yolks
1 cup (250 ml/8 fl oz) milk

➤ CHILL ICE CREAM machine or line a 20 x 30 cm (8 x 12 inch) rectangular tin with plastic wrap and freeze.

1 Combine coffee beans and cream in medium pan. Stir over medium heat until mixture just starts to boil. Add the chocolate and remove from the heat. Set the mixture aside for 1 minute before stirring.

2 Combine sugar and egg yolks in large bowl; whisk until slightly thickened, then whisk in milk. Gradually add coffee mixture with beans. Whisk until smooth. Strain beans from mixture; discard beans.

3 Return coffee-cream mixture to pan; stir over low heat until mixture thickens and will coat the back of a spoon. Remove from heat; cool.

4 Place mixture in ice-cream machine and churn until firm or pour into prepared tin and freeze until just firm. Transfer to large bowl and beat with electric beaters until thick. Return to tin; cover with plastic wrap and refreeze until firm. Repeat, beating once more before transferring to a container for storage in freezer. Serve ice cream scoops with frosted rose petals (see Note).

COOK'S FILE

Storage time: Store in the freezer for up to seven days.

Hint: For an even richer ice cream, add 1/4 cup (45 g/1 1/2 oz) chocolate dots before churning.

Note: *To frost rose petals:* lightly whisk 1 egg white; dip the required quantity of clean petals in egg white (or brush lightly with a paintbrush), then sprinkle with sugar. Shake off excess sugar and place on a paper-lined tray to dry.

CHOCOLATE FONDUE

Preparation time: 15 minutes
Total cooking time: 8 minutes
Serves 6

250 g (8 oz) strawberries
2 kiwi fruit, peeled, halved,
    sliced
2 apples, cored and cut into
    2 cm (³/4 inch) cubes

1 banana, peeled, thickly sliced
250 g (8 oz) marshmallows

Fondue
250 g (8 oz) dark cooking
    chocolate, chopped
¹/2 cup (125 ml/4 fl oz) thick
    cream
2–3 teaspoons orange flavoured
    liqueur

➤CUT STRAWBERRIES in half.
1 Thread fruit and marshmallows

alternately onto skewers.
2 To make Fondue: Melt chocolate
and cream in medium heatproof bowl;
stand over a pan of simmering water.
Stir until melted and smooth; cool.
3 Add liqueur to mixture. Transfer
chocolate mixture to warmed serving
bowl. Serve warm with fruit skewers.

COOK'S FILE

Storage time: Fondue can be
prepared several hours in advance.
Reheat gently before serving.

CHOCOLATE CREPES WITH GRAND MARNIER SAUCE

Preparation time: 40 minutes
Total cooking time: 10–15 minutes
Makes 8–10

2 eggs
2 tablespoons caster sugar
1/2 cup (60 g/2 oz) plain flour
1 tablespoon cocoa powder
1 cup (250 ml/8 fl oz) milk
3 oranges

Sauce
160 g (5 1/4 oz) dark chocolate, chopped
3/4 cup (185 ml/6 fl oz) cream
2–3 tablespoons Grand Marnier

1/2 cup (125 g/4 oz) sour cream or crème fraîche
75 g (2 1/2 oz) white chocolate, grated
250 g (8 oz) punnet blueberries

➤ WHISK EGGS and sugar in large jug until combined.

1 Gradually whisk in sifted flour and cocoa, alternately with milk, until batter is combined and free of lumps. Cover with plastic wrap and stand for 30 minutes. Cut a 1 cm (1/2 inch) slice from the ends of each orange. Cut the skin away in a circular motion, cutting only deep enough to remove all white membrane and skin. Cut the flesh into segments between each membrane. (Do this over a bowl to catch any juice.) Place the segments in a bowl with the juice. Cover with plastic wrap and refrigerate.

2 Heat a 20 cm (8 inch) non-stick pan over medium heat. Brush lightly with a little melted butter. Pour 2–3 tablespoons of crepe batter into pan; swirl evenly over base. Cook over medium heat 1 minute or until underside is cooked. Turn crepe over and cook the other side. Transfer the crepe to a plate; cover with a tea-towel to keep warm. Repeat process with remaining batter, greasing the pan when necessary. (This mixture should make between 8–10 crepes, depending on their thickness.)

3 To make Sauce: Drain oranges; reserve juice. Combine juice in pan with chocolate, cream and Grand Marnier. Stir over low heat until chocolate has melted and mixture is smooth.

To assemble crepes: Place 1 heaped teaspoon of sour cream or crème fraîche on a quarter of each crepe. Sprinkle with grated white chocolate. Fold crepe in half, and in half again to make a wedge shape. Place two crepes on each serving plate. Spoon warm sauce over crepes and serve with orange segments and blueberries. If preferred, crepes and sauce can be prepared and cooked several hours in advance. Reheat gently, fill and assemble just before serving.

1

2

3

CHOCOLATE FLAVOURED MOCHA AND BERRY TRIFLE

Preparation time: 35 minutes +
  3 hours refrigeration
Total cooking time: Nil
Serves 6–8

250 g (8 oz) light cream cheese
$2/3$ cup (170 ml/$5^1/2$ fl oz) cream
4 eggs, separated
250 g (8 oz) mascarpone cheese
80 g ($2^2/3$ oz) white chocolate,
  grated
$1/3$ cup (90 g/3 oz) caster sugar
2 cups (500 ml/16 fl oz) strong
  black coffee
1 tablespoon soft brown sugar
$1/4$ cup (60 ml/2 fl oz) Tia Maria
  or chocolate-based liqueur
1 tablespoon rum or brandy
500 g (1 lb) savoiardi (sponge
  finger) biscuits
300 g ($9^2/3$ oz) frozen or fresh
  raspberries
$1/4$ cup (30 g/1 oz) dark cocoa
  powder
whipped cream and extra cocoa
  powder, to serve

►PLACE CREAM cheese in large mixing bowl; beat until smooth.

1 Add cream and yolks; beat a further 2 minutes or until slightly thickened. Using a metal spoon, fold in mascarpone cheese and chocolate. Stir until just combined and mixture is smooth. (Do not overbeat or the mascarpone will curdle.)

2 Beat egg whites in small mixing bowl until stiff peaks form. Add sugar gradually, beating constantly after each addition, until mixture is thick and glossy and sugar is dissolved. Fold egg white mixture into cheese mixture, stirring until smooth. Combine coffee, sugar, liqueur and rum or brandy in medium bowl. Quickly dip one-third of the sponge fingers into coffee mixture.

3 Arrange biscuits in base of 8-cup capacity serving bowl. Sprinkle with 1 tablespoon cocoa and one-third of the raspberries. Spread with one-third of the cheese mixture. Repeat layering twice more with dipped biscuits, cocoa, raspberries and cheese mixture. Cover and refrigerate several hours or overnight, to allow the flavours to develop. To serve, top with freshly whipped cream and sprinkle with extra cocoa powder.

COOK'S FILE

Storage: Trifle can be made up to two days in advance. Store covered in the refrigerator.

Hint: Trifle can also be made in small individual serving bowls or dishes.

1

2

3

CHOCOLATE BREAD AND BUTTER PUDDING

Preparation time: 25 minutes
Total cooking time: 40–45 minutes
Serves 4–6

60 g (2 oz) butter
6 slices fruit-loaf bread
1/2 cup (125 ml/4 fl oz) milk
2 cups (500 ml/16 fl oz) thick
    cream
1/2 cup (125 g/4 oz) caster sugar
100 g (3 1/3 oz) dark cooking
    chocolate, chopped

4 eggs, lightly beaten
1/2 cup (90 g/3 oz) dark choc
    bits
2 tablespoons golden syrup

►PREHEAT OVEN to warm 160°C (315°F/Gas 2–3). Brush a 4-cup capacity baking dish with oil or melted butter.
1 Spread butter on bread. Cut bread into diagonal quarters. Place bread in dish in single layer, overlapping it.
2 Combine milk, cream and sugar in medium pan, stir over low heat until sugar dissolves. Bring to boil, remove from heat. Add chocolate; stir mixture until melted and smooth. Cool

slightly; gradually whisk in eggs.
3 Pour half the custard mixture over bread, stand 10 minutes or until bread absorbs most of the liquid. Pour over remaining custard mixture. Sprinkle with choc bits. Drizzle with golden syrup. Bake 40–45 minutes or until set and slightly puffed and golden. Serve warm or cold with cream or ice-cream.

COOK'S FILE

Hint: Substitute plain white bread and 1/4 cup (35 g/1 1/4 oz) sultanas or currants for the fruit-loaf bread if it is unavailable.

CHOCOLATE CREME CARAMEL

Preparation time : 25 minutes
Total cooking time: 45 minutes
Makes 4

$^3/_4$ cup (185 g/6 oz) caster sugar
$^3/_4$ cup (185 ml/6 fl oz) water

Custard
4 egg yolks
$^1/_4$ cup (60 g/2 oz) caster sugar
$1^1/_4$ cups (315 ml/10 fl oz) milk
$^3/_4$ cup (185 ml/6 fl oz) cream
**150 g ($4^3/_4$ oz) dark cooking
    chocolate, chopped**

➤PREHEAT OVEN to warm 160°C
(315°F/Gas 2–3).
1 Combine sugar and water in small
pan; stir over low heat without boiling
until sugar has dissolved. Bring to
boil; reduce heat then simmer until
syrup just turns golden.
2 Quickly pour toffee into four 1-cup
capacity ramekin dishes or heatproof
moulds. Allow to set.
3 To make Custard: Whisk egg
yolks and sugar until combined and
slightly thickened. Combine milk and
cream in medium pan. Bring to boil,
then remove from heat. Add chocolate; stir until melted. Gradually
whisk into egg mixture. Pour custard
through a fine strainer into a large
jug. Pour into toffee-lined dishes.
4 Place serving dishes in a large baking dish. Pour in enough hot water to
come half way up the sides of the
dishes. Bake 45 minutes or until
custard is just set. (Custard will set
more on standing.) Remove from heat;
stand until cooled. Refrigerate
overnight. Run a knife around the
inside-edge of each dish before
turning out onto serving plates. Serve
plain or with whipped cream and
broken toffee pieces, if desired.

COOK'S FILE

Storage time: This dish best eaten
immediately.
Variation: Add $^1/_3$ cup (50 g/$1^2/_3$ oz)
of grated dark chocolate to custard
instead of melted chocolate. This will
give the dish a crunchy texture. A few
drops of vanilla essence can also be
added to the custard.

CHOCOLATE SHORTBREAD STACKS

Preparation time: 20 minutes
Total cooking time: 15 minutes
Makes 6

1½ cups (185 g/6 oz) plain flour
⅓ cup (40 g/1⅓ oz) cocoa
    powder
¾ cup (90 g/3 oz) icing sugar
225 g (7¼ oz) butter, chopped
2 egg yolks
1 teaspoon vanilla essence
1 cup (250 ml/8 fl oz) cream,
    whipped
250 g (8 oz) fresh strawberries,
    quartered
1 tablespoon icing sugar, extra
1 tablespoon cocoa powder,
    extra

Berry Sauce
250 g (8 oz) fresh or frozen
    strawberries
1 tablespoon caster sugar
1–2 tablespoons water

➤PREHEAT OVEN to hot 210°C
(415°F/Gas 6). Line two oven trays
with baking paper.
1 Place flour, cocoa, icing sugar and
butter in food processor. Process
30 seconds or until mixture is fine and
crumbly. Add yolks and essence;
process until mixture comes together.
Knead gently on a floured surface
until just smooth.
2 Roll pastry between two layers of
baking paper to 5 mm (¼ inch) thick.
Using a 7 cm (2¾ inch) fluted round
cutter, cut 18 rounds from the pastry.
Place on prepared trays. Bake for
8 minutes or until cooked through.
3 Place a biscuit on serving plate, top
with a little cream and some berries.
Top with a second biscuit followed by

cream and berries. Top with a third
biscuit. Repeat with remaining
ingredients to make another 5 stacks.
Dust each with extra sifted cocoa and
icing sugar. Serve with Berry Sauce.
4 To make Berry Sauce: Process
berries and sugar until smooth, stir in

enough water to make a pouring consistency. Strain seeds, if desired.

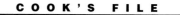
COOK'S FILE

Storage time: Biscuits can be made
a day ahead. Assemble them just
before serving.

NUT MERINGUE WITH MILK CHOCOLATE AND STRAWBERRIES

Preparation time: 30 minutes
Total cooking time: 40 minutes
Serves 10–12

6 egg whites
1¹/₂ cups (375 g/12 oz) caster
    sugar
1 teaspoon cream of tartar
1 teaspoon lemon juice
¹/₃ cup (60 g/2 oz) ground
    almonds
¹/₃ cup (35 g/1¹/₄ oz) ground
    hazelnuts
3 teaspoons cornflour

Filling
250 g (8 oz) milk chocolate
    melts
60 g (2 oz) butter
¹/₃ cup (80 ml/2³/₄ fl oz) cream
1¹/₄ cups (315 ml/10 fl oz)
    cream, whipped
250 g (8 oz) strawberries,
    quartered

Caraque Curls
100 g (3¹/₃ oz) dark chocolate
    melts, melted
100 g (3¹/₃ oz) white chocolate
    melts, melted

► PREHEAT OVEN to slow 150°C (300°F/Gas 2). Line three oven trays with baking paper. Draw a 21 cm (8¹/₂ inch) circle on each sheet.
1 Beat egg whites in large bowl until soft peaks form. Gradually add sugar, beating well after each addition; beat until sugar has dissolved and mixture is thick and glossy. Fold in cream of tartar and lemon juice. Using a metal spoon, fold in almonds, hazelnuts and cornflour until just combined.

2 Divide mixture between the trays, spread evenly onto the circles using the traced paper as a guide. Bake for 40 minutes or until meringue is firm and crisp. Turn off oven; cool the meringues in oven with door ajar.
To make Filling: Melt chocolate and butter in small pan, stir in cream; mix until smooth. Cool until mixture thickens to a spreadable consistency. Transfer mixture to bowl. Beat, using electric mixer, until creamy.
3 Place a meringue disc on serving plate; spread with half the filling. Top with one-third of the whipped cream

and one-third of the strawberries. Top with another disc; repeat with remaining filling, half the cream and one-third of the strawberries. Top with remaining disc. Spread with remaining cream and decorate with remaining strawberries and Caraque Curls. Refrigerate until ready to serve. Dust with sifted icing sugar, if desired.
To make Caraque Curls: Spread alternate bands of melted dark and white chocolate onto cool flat work surface. Allow to just set. Slowly run a large knife over the chocolate to produce long curls.

1

2

3

PETITS FOURS

CHOCOLATE MERINGUE KISSES

Preparation time: 20 minutes
Total cooking time: 40 minutes
Makes 25

2 egg whites
$^{1}/_{2}$ cup (125 g/4 oz) caster sugar
$^{1}/_{4}$ teaspoon ground cinnamon

Filling
125 g (4 oz) dark chocolate
   melts
$^{1}/_{3}$ cup (90 g/3 oz) sour cream

➤ PREHEAT OVEN to slow 150°C (300°F/Gas 2). Line two oven trays with baking paper.
1 Using electric beaters, beat egg whites in small bowl until soft peaks form. Gradually add sugar, beating well after each addition. Beat until sugar has dissolved and mixture is thick and glossy. Add cinnamon and beat until just combined.
2 Transfer mixture to piping bag fitted with 1 cm ($^{1}/_{2}$ inch) fluted tube. Pipe small stars of 1.5 cm ($^{5}/_{8}$ inch) diameter onto prepared trays 3 cm ($1^{1}/_{4}$ inches) apart. Bake 30 minutes or until pale and crisp. Turn off oven; cool in oven with door ajar.

3 To make Filling: Place chocolate and sour cream in a small heatproof bowl; stand bowl over pan of simmering water. Stir until chocolate has melted and mixture is smooth. Remove from heat; cool slightly. Sandwich meringues together with Filling. Dust with cocoa to serve, if desired. Serve immediately.

COOK'S FILE

Storage time: Unfilled meringues can be made several days ahead. Store in airtight container, between sheets of greaseproof paper.
Variations: Use white chocolate instead of dark chocolate. Use other ground spices in meringues such as ground cloves, allspice or nutmeg.
Notes: When making meringue ensure that the bowl is completely clean and dry. Even a tiny trace of grease will prevent the egg whites whipping. If possible use a copper bowl for mixing. Meringues should be cooked slowly—they are dried rather than baked. The ideal texture for meringue is crunchy on the outside, yet soft inside. Once mixed with other ingredients, particularly those containing dairy products, the meringue will begin to soften.
Hint: Unfilled meringues can be used as decorations on a cake.

RUM TRUFFLES

Preparation time: 20 minutes
+ 20 minutes refrigeration
Total cooking time: 1 minute
Makes about 25

200 g (6$^{1}/_{2}$ oz) dark cooking
    chocolate, finely chopped
$^{1}/_{4}$ cup (60 ml/2 fl oz) cream
30 g (1 oz) butter
50 g (1$^{2}/_{3}$ oz) chocolate cake
    crumbs
2 teaspoons dark rum

$^{1}/_{2}$ cup (95 g/3$^{1}/_{4}$ oz) chocolate
    sprinkles

►LINE AN oven tray with foil.
1 Place chocolate in a medium bowl.
Combine cream and butter in a small
pan; stir over low heat until the
butter melts and mixture is just
boiling. Pour hot cream mixture over
the chocolate; stir until chocolate
melts and mixture is smooth.
2 Stir in cake crumbs and rum;
combine well. Refrigerate 20 minutes,
stirring occasionally or until it is just
firm enough to handle. Roll heaped

teaspoons of mixture into balls.
3 Spread chocolate sprinkles on a
sheet of greaseproof paper. Roll each
truffle in sprinkles, then place on the
prepared tray. Refrigerate 30 minutes
or until firm. Serve in small paper
patty cups, if desired.

COOK'S FILE

Variations: Other brown spirits can
be used in place of rum—brandy or
whisky, for example.

Truffles can also be rolled in dark
cocoa powder. (This is available in
most delicatessens.)

1

2

3

KIRSCH CHOCOLATE CHERRIES

Preparation time: 20 minutes +
20 minutes refrigeration
Total cooking time: Nil
Makes 25

1 egg white
125 g (4 oz) dark chocolate
$^1/_2$ cup (95 g/3$^1/_4$ oz) ground
   almonds

1 tablespoon kirsch
2 tablespoons icing sugar
25 glacé cherries
$^1/_4$ cup (30 g/1 oz) cocoa
$^1/_4$ cup (30 g/1 oz) drinking
   chocolate

►LIGHTLY BEAT egg white.
1 Finely grate chocolate over sheet of greaseproof paper. Combine chocolate, almonds, kirsch and icing sugar in a medium bowl. Slowly stir in enough egg white to bind the mixture.

Refrigerate 20 minutes.
2 Flatten 2 level teaspoons of mixture in the palm of your hand; work gently to enclose a glacé cherry; smooth to a round ball.
3 Roll balls in sifted combined cocoa and drinking chocolate. Place between layers of greaseproof paper in an airtight container. Refrigerate until hard.

COOK'S FILE

Storage time: Cherries can be made and refrigerated a week in advance.

2

3

1

WALNUT CHOCOLATES

Preparation time: 30 minutes
+ 20 minutes standing
Total cooking time: 2–3 minutes
Makes 30

100 g (3¹/₃ oz) walnut pieces
¹/₂ cup (60 g/2 oz) icing sugar
2 teaspoons egg white

200 g (6¹/₂ oz) dark chocolate
30 walnut halves

➤PROCESS WALNUT pieces in food processor until fine.
1 Add sifted icing sugar and egg white and process to a moist paste. Cover and refrigerate 20 minutes.
2 Roll teaspoons of walnut paste into balls; flatten slightly with your finger. Set aside. Place chocolate in heatproof bowl; stand bowl over pan of simmering water. Stir until smooth and melted.
3 Dip walnut rounds in melted chocolate. Place rounds on greaseproof paper or foil. Press walnut halves gently into the top of each round and allow to set.

COOK'S FILE

Storage time: Can be made up to four days in advance.

1

2

3

LIQUEUR PRALINE TRUFFLES

Preparation time: 30 minutes
Total cooking time: 15 minutes
Makes 34

1/3 cup (50 g/1²/3 oz) blanched
    almonds, toasted
1/3 cup (45 g/1¹/2 oz) hazelnuts,
    toasted
2/3 cup (160 g/5¹/4 oz) caster
    sugar
1/3 cup (80 ml/2³/4 fl oz) water
250 g (8 oz) dark cooking
    chocolate
60 g (2 oz) butter
1/3 cup (80 ml/2³/4 fl oz) cream
2 egg yolks

1 tablespoon coffee flavoured
    liqueur (Kahlua)
1/4 cup (30 g/1 oz) cocoa powder

►LINE AN OVEN tray with baking
paper.
1 Place nuts onto prepared tray.
Combine sugar and water in small
pan. Stir over low heat, without
boiling, until sugar dissolves. Bring to
boil, reduce heat and simmer until
mixture turns a light golden colour.
Pour hot toffee over nuts and allow to
set hard.
2 Break toffee into small pieces. Chop
or process in food processor until fine.
Set the praline aside.
3 Melt chocolate and butter in a
small pan, stirring over low heat until
chocolate has melted and mixture is

smooth. Stir in cream, yolks and
liqueur. Stir until smooth; cool to
room temperature. Stir in the
processed praline.
4 Shape 1¹/2 teaspoons of mixture
into balls. Roll in sifted cocoa powder
just before serving.

COOK'S FILE

Variation: Use pecans, pistachios or
walnuts in place of almonds and
hazelnuts.

CHOC AND ORANGE MARSHMALLOW FUDGE

Preparation time: 25 minutes
Total cooking time: 10 minutes
Makes 35 pieces

100 g (3$\frac{1}{3}$ oz) pink and white marshmallows
$\frac{1}{4}$ cup (60 ml/2 fl oz) orange juice
90 g (3 oz) unsalted butter, cut into small cubes
375 g (12 oz) dark chocolate, roughly chopped
$\frac{1}{2}$ teaspoon vanilla essence
1 teaspoon grated orange rind
185 g (6 oz) walnuts, roughly chopped

Candied Citrus Peel
rind of 1 orange
$\frac{1}{2}$ cup (125 g/4 oz) caster sugar
$\frac{1}{4}$ cup (60 ml/2 fl oz) water

➤ LINE THE base of a 20 x 30 cm (8 x 12 inch) recangular or lamington tin with baking paper, extending paper over the long sides.

1 Combine marshmallows, orange juice and butter in a medium heavy-based pan. Cook over low heat for 5 minutes, stirring occasionally, until marshmallows have melted. Remove mixture from heat; cool slightly. Add chocolate, vanilla essence, orange rind and walnuts, stirring until chocolate has melted and mixture is smooth.

2 Pour into prepared tin and smooth surface. Leave to set. When firm, cut

into small diamond-shaped pieces. Top with Candied Citrus Peel.

3 To make Candied Citrus Peel: Cut rind into fine strips. Combine rind, caster sugar and water in small pan and stir over low heat until sugar has dissolved. Bring to boil; reduce heat. Simmer, uncovered, for 5 minutes without stirring. Remove rind from the pan with tongs. Transfer to a wire rack to drain. Cool completely.

COOK'S FILE

Storage time: Fudge can be made up to a week in advance. Keep refrigerated. Fudge keeps well and makes an attractive gift. Wrap in tissue paper or rice paper.
Hint: Reserve candied rind syrup and use as a sauce on ice-cream.

CHOCOLATE FRUIT AND NUT PATE

Preparation time: 20 minutes
Total cooking time: 3–5 minutes
Makes about 40 slices

25 g ($\frac{3}{4}$ oz) butter
$\frac{1}{2}$ cup (160 g/5$\frac{1}{4}$ oz) condensed milk
300 g (9$\frac{2}{3}$ oz) dark choc bits
2 teaspoons orange liqueur

$\frac{1}{4}$ cup (35 g/1$\frac{1}{4}$ oz) hazelnuts, toasted
$\frac{1}{4}$ cup (40 g/1$\frac{1}{3}$ oz) macadamia nuts, toasted
$\frac{1}{4}$ cup (25 g/$\frac{3}{4}$ oz) pecans
2–3 tablespoons flaked almonds, toasted
4 glacé apricots, chopped
2 glacé figs, chopped

➤ LINE A 26 x 8 cm (10$\frac{1}{2}$ x 3 inch) bar tin with foil.

1 Combine butter, condensed milk,

choc bits and liqueur in pan. Stir over low heat until chocolate has melted and mixture is smooth. Transfer to a bowl.

2 Add nuts and fruit to chocolate mixture; stir to combine. Spoon into prepared tin; smooth surface. Tap tin on bench to remove any air bubbles. Refrigerate 2 hours or until firm.

3 Turn pâté out onto board; remove foil. Cut into thin slices to serve. Pâté can be made up to two weeks in advance. Refrigerate in warm weather and remove just before serving.

Choc and Orange Marshmallow Fudge (top) and Chocolate Fruit and Nut Pâté

CHOCOLATE NUT SWIRLS

Preparation time: 45 minutes
Total cooking time: 12 minutes
 each tray
Makes about 40

1 cup (125 g/4 oz) plain flour
1/2 cup (60 g/2 oz) icing sugar
1/4 cup (30 g/1 oz) cocoa powder
80 g (2²/3 oz) butter, chopped
1 egg yolk
1 tablespoon water
20 pecans, halved
150 g (4³/4 oz) dark cooking
 chocolate
20 g (²/3 oz) white vegetable
 shortening (copha)

Ganache
125 g (4 oz) dark cooking
 chocolate
40 g (1¹/3 oz) unsalted butter
2 tablespoons cream

➤PREHEAT OVEN to moderate 180°C (350°F/Gas 4). Line two oven trays with baking paper.
1 Place flour, sugar, cocoa and butter in food processor. Process for 30 seconds or until mixture resembles fine crumbs. Add egg yolk and water, process until mixture just comes together.
2 Turn dough onto lightly floured surface; press together gently until smooth. Cut dough in half; wrap one half in plastic wrap and set aside. Roll out other half on baking paper to 4 mm thickness. Using a biscuit cutter or sharp knife cut into 3 cm (1¹/4 inch) squares. Lift squares onto prepared trays. Bake 10–12 minutes. Transfer to wire rack to cool. Repeat with remaining biscuit dough.
3 To make Ganache: Combine

chocolate, butter and cream in small pan, stir over low heat until chocolate has melted and mixture is smooth. Refrigerate until just starting to set; stir until smooth. Transfer mixture to a piping bag fitted with a 5 mm (¹/4 inch) fluted nozzle. Pipe a swirl of Ganache onto each biscuit. Insert a nut into centre of swirl. Allow to set until firm. (Refrigerate if necessary.) Combine chocolate and shortening in

small heatproof bowl and stir over pan of simmering water until melted and smooth. Holding biscuit by its top, dip biscuit bases in chocolate; place on foil trays to set.

Storage time: Store biscuits in an airtight container up to two weeks.
Variation: Use cherries, glacé fruit or other nuts instead of pecans.

1

2

3

APRICOT CHOCOLATES

Preparation time: 25 minutes
Total cooking time: 5 minutes
Makes 40

175 g (5²/₃ oz) dark chocolate,
   roughly chopped
200 g (6¹/₂ oz) dried apricots
20 blanched almonds, halved

➤LINE AN OVEN tray with baking paper.

1 Place chocolate in a small heat-proof bowl; stand bowl over a pan of simmering water until chocolate has melted.

2 Dip half of each apricot in melted chocolate; drain excess, place on prepared tray. Top with almond half and allow to set. Place remaining chocolate over simmering water to re-melt.

3 Spoon remaining chocolate into paper icing bag. Seal end; snip off tip. Pipe chocolate across apricots in a zig-zag pattern. Allow to set.

COOK'S FILE

Storage time: Apricot Chocolates can be made up to a week in advance. Store in an airtight container.
Hint: Other dried fruit can be used in place of apricots.

1

2

3

GLACE FRUIT ROUNDS

Preparation time: 25 minutes
+ 2 hours standing
Total cooking time: 2–3 minutes
Makes 70

$^{1}/_{3}$ cup (70 g/2$^{1}/_{3}$ oz) glacé
   cherries, finely chopped
$^{1}/_{4}$ cup (55 g/1$^{3}/_{4}$ oz) finely
   chopped glacé pineapple
$^{1}/_{4}$ cup (60 g/2 oz) glacé
   apricots, finely chopped
2 tablespoons glacé ginger,
   finely chopped

1 tablespoon brandy
185 g (6 oz) milk chocolate,
   roughly chopped

➤ LINE A flat or oven tray with baking paper.

1 Combine glacé fruit and brandy in a small bowl. Stand 2 hours.

2 Place chocolate in a medium heatproof bowl; stand bowl over a pan of simmering water until melted. Place $^{1}/_{2}$ teaspoons of melted chocolate on prepared tray and shape into circles.

3 Quickly place $^{1}/_{4}$ teaspoon of fruit mixture on top of each circle and press gently. Place in refrigerator and allow to set. Remove rounds gently from paper using a flat knife.

COOK'S FILE

Storage time: Fruit Rounds can be made up to a week in advance. Store chocolates in an airtight container in a cool dry place. Refrigerate in warmer weather and bring to room temperature before serving.

Variations: Try a combination of chopped nuts in conjunction with soaked glacé fruits. Brandy can be replaced with 1 tablespoon lemon juice, if preferred.

VIENNESE CHOCOLATE DIPPED STRAWBERRIES

Preparation time: 30 minutes
Total cooking time: 5 minutes
Makes 12

12 medium strawberries
155 g (5 oz) white chocolate,
 roughly chopped
60 g (2 oz) dark chocolate,
 roughly chopped

➤LINE A flat tray or board with baking paper.

1 Clean strawberries lightly with a pastry brush. Do not remove hulls.

2 Place white chocolate in a medium heatproof bowl; stand bowl over a pan of simmering water until chocolate has melted and mixture is smooth. Remove from heat. Holding the strawberries by their tops, dip approximately two-thirds into the chocolate. Drain excess, then place on prepared tray or board. Allow to set.

3 Place dark chocolate in a small heatproof bowl; stand bowl over a pan of simmering water until chocolate has melted and mixture is smooth; allow to cool slightly. Dip a third of the coated strawberries in dark chocolate. Replace on paper tray or board and refrigerate until required.

COOK'S FILE

Storage time: Chocolate coated strawberries will keep up to 12 hours in refrigerator.

1

2

3

TEARDROP CHOCOLATE CHERRY MOUSSE CUPS

Preparation time: 1 hour
Total cooking time: Nil
Makes about 24

2 x 28 x 21.5 cm (11 x 8$^{1}/_{2}$ inch)
    (A4) transparency sheets (see
    Note)
200 g (6$^{1}/_{2}$ oz) dark chocolate
    melts
$^{3}/_{4}$ cup (150 g/4$^{3}/_{4}$ oz) stoneless
    black cherries, well drained

Chocolate Mousse
60 g (2 oz) dark cooking
    chocolate, melted
1 tablespoon cream
1 egg yolk
$^{1}/_{2}$ teaspoon gelatine
2 teaspoons water
$^{1}/_{3}$ cup (80 ml/2$^{3}/_{4}$ fl oz) cream
1 egg white

➤ CUT CLEAR transparency film
into 4 x 11 cm (1$^{1}/_{2}$ x 4$^{1}/_{2}$ inch) rectangles. Line flat tray with baking paper.

1 Place chocolate melts in small bowl; stand over a pan of simmering water. Stir until chocolate has melted and mixture is smooth. Using a palette or flat-bladed knife spread a little of the chocolate over one transparency rectangle. Just before chocolate starts to set, bring the short edges together to form a teardrop shape. (Leave transparency film attached.) Hold together with fingers until shape holds by itself and will stand up. Repeat with remaining chocolate and transparency rectangles. (Chocolate will need to be re-melted several times during this process. To do this, place bowl over simmering water again.)

2 Spoon approximately 1$^{1}/_{2}$ teaspoons of chocolate on prepared tray 3 cm (1$^{1}/_{4}$ inches) apart. Spread chocolate into an oval shape approximately 5 cm (2 inches) long. Sit a teardrop in the centre of each oval; press down gently. Allow to almost set.

3 Using a sharp small knife or scalpel, cut around outer edge of each teardrop. Allow cups to set completely before lifting away from baking paper. Carefully break away excess chocolate from bases to form a neat edge on the base. Carefully peel away transparency strips. Set cups aside. Cut cherries into quarters; allow to drain on paper towels.

4 To make Chocolate Mousse: Combine chocolate, cream and yolk in medium bowl; mix until smooth. Sprinkle gelatine over water in small bowl, stand bowl over boiling water until gelatine dissolves. Stir into chocolate mixture.

5 Working quickly, so that gelatine does not set, beat cream in medium bowl with electric beaters until soft peaks form; fold into chocolate mixture. Using electric beaters, beat egg white in dry clean bowl until soft peaks form. Fold egg whites into chocolate mixture.

6 Place a few pieces of cherry inside the base of each teardrop cup. Spoon chocolate mixture over cherries. (Fill cups to slightly over the brim as mousse will drop a little during setting.) Refrigerate until set.

COOK'S FILE

Storage time: Chocolate cups can be made a day ahead. Fill with mousse several hours in advance.

Note: Transparency sheets are made from firm acetate which will hold chocolate upright and firm as it sets. They are available from newsagents or art supplies shops. Other materials cannot be used instead of acetate.

1

2

3

4

5

6

TROPICAL TRUFFLES

Preparation time: 35 minutes
Total cooking time: 10 minutes
Makes 20

$\frac{1}{2}$ cup (80 g/$2^2/3$ oz)
    macadamia nuts, finely
    chopped
2 tablespoons finely chopped
    crystalised pawpaw
2 teaspoons lemon juice
2 tablespoons cream
90 g (3 oz) white chocolate,
    finely chopped

$\frac{1}{2}$ cup (45 g/$1^1/2$ oz) desiccated
    coconut

➤SPREAD MACADAMIA nuts on
flat oven tray and toast in preheated
moderate 180°C (350°F/Gas 4) oven
for 3–5 minutes or until golden.
1 Combine pawpaw and lemon juice
in a small bowl. Stand 10 minutes.
Add toasted macadamia nuts and stir
to combine.
2 Heat cream in a small pan over
medium heat until boiling. Add
chocolate, remove from heat and stir
until chocolate melts and the mixture
is smooth. Transfer to a small bowl.

Stir in pawpaw and lemon juice and
refrigerate 20 minutes or until firm
enough to handle.
3 Roll heaped teaspoons of mixture
into balls. Roll balls in desiccated
coconut and place in an airtight container between sheets of greaseproof
paper. Refrigerate until set.

COOK'S FILE

Variations: Add $\frac{1}{4}$ cup (40 g/
$1^1/3$ oz) grated white chocolate to
coconut for extra taste and texture.

Add 1 tablespoon chopped glacè
ginger or 1 tablespoon dried apricot to
truffle mixture.

1

2

3

1

2

3

4

CHOCOLATE CUPS WITH CARAMEL

Preparation time: 40 minutes
Total cooking time: 5–10 minutes
Makes 24

150 g (4³⁄₄ oz) dark chocolate melts
24 small foil confectionery cups
80 g (2²⁄₃ oz) Mars bar, chopped
¹⁄₄ cup (60 ml/2 fl oz) cream
50 g (1²⁄₃ oz) white chocolate melts

➤ PLACE DARK CHOCOLATE in small heatproof bowl; stand bowl over pan of simmering water. Stir until chocolate has melted and mixture is smooth. Remove from heat.

1 Using a small paint brush, brush a thin layer of chocolate inside foil cases. Stand cases upside-down on wire rack to set. (Return remaining chocolate to pan of simmering water for later use.)

2 Combine Mars bar and cream in small pan; stir over low heat until melted and smooth. Transfer to bowl; stand until just starting to set. Spoon caramel mixture into each cup leaving about 3 mm of space at the top.

3 Spoon reserved melted chocolate into caramel cases and allow chocolate to set. Melt white chocolate in the same way as dark chocolate. Place in a small paper piping bag.

Drizzle patterns over the cups. Carefully peel away foil when set.

COOK'S FILE

Storage time: Caramel cups can be made three days ahead. Store in airtight container in cool place.

Hint: If dark chocolate is still unset when piping with white chocolate, tap cups gently on the bench. The white chocolate will set into the dark, leaving a flat surface.

CHOCOLATE COATED ORANGE PEEL

Preparation time: 35 minutes
  + overnight standing
Total cooking time: 35 minutes
Makes about 40

2 large thick-skinned
    oranges
1 cup (250 ml/8 fl oz) water
1 cup (250 g/8 oz) caster sugar
150 g (4³/4 oz) dark cooking
    chocolate
20 g (²/3 oz) white vegetable
    shortening (copha)

►CUT ORANGES into quarters. Carefully remove peel in large sections, removing any excess pith with a sharp knife.

1 Using a 2 cm (³/4 inch) biscuit cutter or a small sharp knife, cut the peel into rounds or shapes. Drop the rounds into a pan of boiling water, simmer for 5 minutes; drain. Repeat twice more using fresh boiling water each time you do it.

2 Combine water and caster sugar in pan; stir over low heat without boiling until sugar dissolves. Add orange shapes; bring to boil, reduce heat and simmer 5–10 minutes, stirring occasionally, or until the peel be-comes translucent.

3 Transfer shapes to large wire rack to drain. To dry thoroughly, stand peel overnight, loosely covered with foil.

4 Combine chocolate and vegetable shortening in small pan; stir over low heat until melted and smooth. Using two forks, dip peel in chocolate to coat; drain excess. Stand shapes on foil-lined tray until set.

COOK'S FILE

Storage time: Chocolate coated peel can be made up to two days in advance. Store in airtight container in cool place or refrigerator.

Variation: Use this recipe for other types of citrus peel, such as grapefruit, mandarin or lime. Several different types of peel served in the same sweet dish makes an attractive after-dinner treat.

If time is limited, peel can be cut into simple thin strips.

CHOCOLATE FRUIT AND NUT FUDGE

Preparation time: 25 minutes
Total cooking time: 8–10 minutes
Makes one 20 cm (8 inch) square slab

500 g (1 lb) icing sugar, sifted
375 ml (12 fl oz) evaporated milk
45 g ($1^{1}/2$ oz) butter
175 g ($5^{2}/3$ oz) dark chocolate
100 g ($3^{1}/3$ oz) coarsley chopped macadamia nuts
$^{1}/4$ cup (30 g/1 oz) sultanas
$^{1}/4$ cup (55 g/$1^{3}/4$ oz) glacé cherries, quartered

►LINE BASE and sides of a deep 20 cm (8 inch) square cake tin with foil, extending foil over two sides. Grease the foil thoroughly with oil or melted butter.

1 Combine sugar, milk and butter in medium heavy-based pan. Stir over low heat, without boiling, until sugar has dissolved and butter has melted. Bring to boil, stirring constantly. Continue stirring 8–10 minutes or until a teaspoon of mixture dropped into cold water forms a soft ball. (If using a candy thermometer, the temperature must reach 115°C (235°F).) Remove from heat immediately.

2 Add coarsely chopped chocolate; stir until chocolate has melted and the mixture is smooth. Transfer mixture to small bowl. Beat 4–5 minutes or until mixture lightens in colour. Quickly fold in the nuts and fruit; mix well until thoroughly combined.

3 Pour mixture into prepared tin; smooth surface. Stand tin on wire rack to allow fudge to set, marking fudge into squares with sharp knife while still warm. When fudge has set and is cool, remove foil and cut into squares or triangles.

COOK'S FILE

Storage time: Keep fudge for up to two weeks in an airtight container. Store carefully between layers of greaseproof paper.

1   2   3

CHOCOLATE LAMINGTONS

Preparation time: 40 minutes
Total cooking time: 20 minutes
Makes 60

4 eggs, separated
²/3 cup (160 g/5¹/4 oz) caster
   sugar
2 tablespoons cocoa powder
¹/4 cup (30 g/1 oz) cornflour
¹/4 cup (30 g/1 oz) plain flour
¹/3 cup (40 g/1¹/3 oz) self-raising
   flour

Chocolate Icing
3 cups (375 g/12 oz) icing sugar

¹/2 cup (60 g/2 oz) cocoa powder
90 g (3 oz) butter, chopped
³/4 cup (185 ml/6 fl oz) boiling
   water
1 tablespoon instant coffee
   powder
3 cups (270 g/8²/3 oz) coconut

➤ PREHEAT OVEN to moderate 180°C (350°F/Gas 4). Line a 20 x 30 cm (8 x 12 inch) rectangular lamington tin with baking paper.

1 Using electric beaters, beat egg whites in small bowl until soft peaks form. Add sugar gradually, beating well after each addition, until sugar has dissolved and mixture is thick and glossy. Add egg yolks; beat until just combined. Transfer mixture to large bowl; gently fold through sifted cocoa and flours.

2 Pour mixture into prepared tin; smooth surface. Bake 20 minutes or until cake is springy to the touch. Stand cake in tin 5 minutes before turning onto wire rack to cool. Cut cake into 3 cm (1¹/4 inch) squares.

3 `To make Chocolate Icing: Sift icing sugar and cocoa into a medium bowl. Stir in combined butter, water and coffee; mix until smooth. Place coconut on large plate. Using two forks, dip cake squares, one at a time, into chocolate icing mixture, roll in coconut, and stand on wire rack. Repeat until all cake has been used. Allow lamingtons to stand at least 1 hour before serving.

CHOCOLATE ALMOND TOFFEE

Preparation time: 15 minutes
Total cooking time: 15–20 minutes
Makes 25

1 cup (90 g/3 oz) flaked
   almonds, toasted
²/3 cup (160 g/5¹/4 oz) caster
   sugar
¹/2 cup (125 ml/4 fl oz) water
150 g (4³/4 oz) dark chocolate
   melts

➤ LINE A FLAT or oven tray with baking paper. Spread almonds over the tray.

1 Combine sugar and water in small pan. Stir over low heat, without boiling, until the sugar dissolves, brushing sides of pan down with a pastry brush dipped in water to remove sugar crystals. Bring mixture to the boil, then reduce heat and simmer 10–15 minutes until mixture turns a golden colour.

2 Working quickly, pour toffee over almonds; allow to set.

3 Cut toffee into thin small wedges or break into pieces. Place chocolate in small heatproof bowl; stand bowl over pan of simmering water until chocolate has melted and mixture is smooth. Remove bowl from heat. Dip wide end of toffee pieces into chocolate. Allow to set on foil-lined tray.

C O O K ' S   F I L E

Storage time: Toffee can be made up to two days in advance. Store in an airtight container between sheets of greaseproof paper.

Hint: Drizzle the toffee pieces with melted chocolate, if preferred.

Chocolate Lamingtons (top) and
Chocolate Almond Toffee

WHITE CAKE TRUFFLES

Preparation time: 25 minutes
Total cooking time: Nil
Makes about 25

2 cups (250 g/8 oz) Madeira
   cake crumbs
2 tablespoons chopped glacé
   orange peel or glacé apricots
1 tablespoon apricot jam

2 tablepoons cream
100 g (3¹/₃ oz) white chocolate,
   melted

Chocolate Coating
150 g (4³/₄ oz) white chocolate
20 g (²/₃ oz) white vegetable
   shortening (copha)

➤LINE AN oven tray with foil.
1 Combine cake crumbs in bowl with chopped peel or apricots, jam, cream and chocolate; mix to a smooth paste.
2 Roll 2 teaspoons of mixture into balls.
3 To make Chocolate Coating: Combine chocolate and shortening in bowl; stand bowl over a pan of simmering water. Stir until melted. Dip balls in chocolate; allow to set on tray. Decorate with gold leaf, if desired.

COOK'S FILE

Storage time: Truffles can be made up to three days ahead.

1

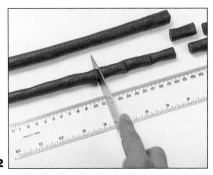

2

3

4

MINI CHOCOLATE SHORTBREADS

Preparation time: 25 minutes
Total cooking time: 12 minutes
Makes about 40

125 g (4 oz) butter, chopped
2 tablespoons rice flour
3/4 cup (90 g/3 oz) plain flour
2 tablespoons icing sugar
1/3 cup drinking chocolate

Topping
150 g (4³/4 oz) white chocolate, melted
30 g (1 oz) white vegetable shortening (copha), chopped

60 g (2 oz) dark cooking chocolate, melted

➤PREHEAT OVEN to warm 160°C (315°F/Gas 2–3). Line two oven trays with baking paper.
1 Combine butter, flours, sugar and drinking chocolate in food processor. Process until mixture comes together.
2 Turn mixture onto lightly floured surface, knead gently until smooth. Divide into four. Roll each portion into a long log 1 cm (1/2 inch) in diameter. Cut logs into 3 cm (1¹/4 inch) lengths. Place lengths on prepared trays. Bake 10–12 minutes. Cool on trays.
3 Combine coarsely chopped white chocolate and vegetable shortening in small heatproof bowl; stand bowl over pan of simmering water. Stir until chocolate has melted and mixture is smooth. Remove from heat.
4 Dip shortbreads in melted chocolate and place on prepared tray to set. Place the dark chocolate in paper piping bag; seal end and snip off tip. Drizzle chocolate over shortbread.

COOK'S FILE

Storage time: Can be stored four days in an airtight container.

CHOCOLATE TUILES

Preparation time: 15 minutes
Total cooking time: 4–6 minutes each
   tray
Makes 12

1 egg white
1/4 cup (60 g/2 oz) caster sugar
2 tablespoons plain flour
30 g (1 oz) butter, melted
1 teaspoon vanilla essence

60 g (2 oz) dark chocolate
   melts, melted

➤ PREHEAT OVEN to moderate 180°C (350°F/Gas 4). Line 2 oven trays with baking paper. Draw two 10 cm (4 inch) circles on each sheet of paper.
1 Combine egg white, sugar, flour, butter and vanilla in bowl; mix to a paste. Place chocolate in a paper piping bag; seal end, snip off tip. Drizzle chocolate over baking paper in swirls following marked circles. Allow chocolate to set.

2 Spread 1 1/2 teaspoons of egg mixture over circles as thinly as possible. Bake circles, one tray at a time, 4–6 minutes or until edges are just turning golden.
3 Remove tray from oven, quickly shape each circle over a rolling pin. Repeat with remaining mixture. Cool tuiles until crisp.

COOK'S FILE

Storage time: Can be made up to two days in advance.

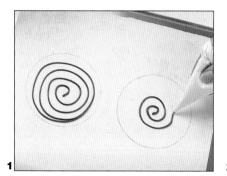

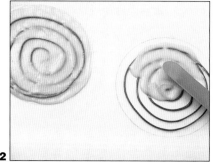

INDEX

Ruler markings (left margin): 1 cm, 2 cm, 3 cm, 4 cm, 5 cm, 6 cm, 7 cm, 8 cm, 9 cm, 10 cm, 11 cm, 12 cm, 13 cm, 14 cm, 15 cm, 16 cm, 17 cm, 18 cm, 19 cm, 20 cm, 21 cm, 22 cm, 23 cm, 24 cm, 25 cm

USEFUL INFORMATION

All our recipes are thoroughly tested in the Australian Test Kitchen. Standard metric measuring cups and spoons approved by Standards Australia are used in the development of our recipes. All cup and spoon measurements are level. We have used eggs with an average weight of 60 g in all recipes. Sizes of cans vary from manufacturer to manufacturer and between countries; use the can size closest to the one suggested in the recipes.

Australian Metric Cup and Spoon Measures

For dry ingredients the standard set of metric measuring cups consists of 1 cup, 1/2 cup, 1/3 cup and 1/4 cup sizes.

For measuring liquids, a transparent, graduated metric measure is available in either a 250 mL cup or a 1 litre jug.

The basic set of metric spoons, used to measure both dry and liquid ingredients, is made up of 1 tablespoon, 1 teaspoon, 1/2 teaspoon and 1/4 teaspoon.

Note: Australian tablespoon equals 20 mL. British, US and NZ tablespoons equal 15 mL for use in liquid measuring. The teaspoon has a 5 mL capacity and is the same for the Australian, British and American markets.

Weights

Metric		Imperial
125 g	=	4 oz
185 g	=	6 oz
250 g	=	8 oz
315 g	=	10 oz
375 g	=	12 oz
440 g	=	14 oz
500 g	=	1 lb
750 g	=	1 1/2 lb
1 kg	=	2 lb
1.5 kg	=	3 lb
2 kg	=	4 lb
2.5 kg	=	5 lb

Measures

1 cm	=	1/2 in
2.5 cm	=	1 in
25 cm	=	10 in
30 cm	=	12 in

Oven Temperatures

Electric	°C	°F
Very slow	120	250
Slow	150	300
Mod. slow	160	325
Moderate	180	350
Mod. hot	210	425
Hot	240	475
Very hot	260	525
Gas	**°C**	**°F**
Very slow	120	250
Slow	150	300
Mod. slow	160	325
Moderate	180	350
Mod. hot	190	375
Hot	200	400
Very hot	230	450

Cup and Spoon Conversions

Australian	British/American
1 tablespoon	3 teaspoons
2 tablespoons	1/4 cup
1/4 cup	1/3 cup
1/3 cup	1/2 cup
1/2 cup	2/3 cup
2/3 cup	3/4 cup
3/4 cup	1 cup
1 cup	1 1/4 cups

Glossary

Australian	British/American	Australian	British/American
cornflour	cornflour/cornstarch	plain flour	plain flour/all-purpose flour
caster sugar	castor sugar/superfine sugar	sultanas	golden raisins/seedless white raisins
essence	essence/extract		
glacé fruit	glacé fruit/candied fruit		

This edition published in 2006 by Bay Books, an imprint of Murdoch Books Pty Limited, Pier 8/9, 23 Hickson Road, Millers Point, NSW 2000, Australia.

Food Editors: Kerrie Ray Jo Anne Calabria **Recipe Development:** Beverley Sutherland Smith, Tracey Port, Maria Sampsonis, Tracy Rutherford **Home Economists:** Maria Sampsonis, Wendy Brodhurst **Food Stylist:** Mary Harris **Food Preparation:** Tracey Port **Photographer:** Jon Bader **Additonal Photography:** Chris Jones, Luis Martin (cover) **Assistant Food Editor:** Tracy Rutherford **Editor:** Amanda Bishop **Designer:** Jacqueline Richards **Picture Librarian:** Dianne Bedford **Production Co-ordinator:** Liz Fitgerald **Chief Executive:** Juliet Rogers **Publisher:** Kay Scarlett

ISBN 1-74045-928-8
Printed by Sing Cheong Printing Co. Ltd. Printed in China.